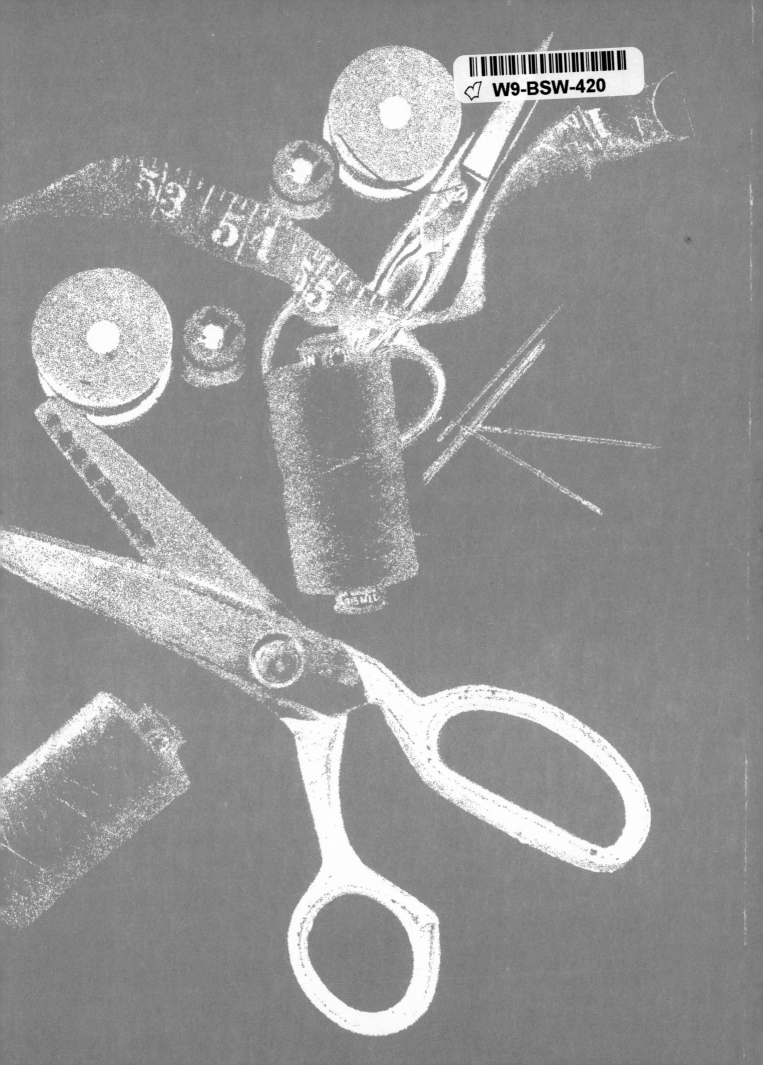

SEWING

All about how to sew for yourself, your family and your home

SEWING

Honor Gillott

Octopus Books

CONTENTS

The publishers would like to thank Simplicity Patterns Limited for their co-operation in producing this book and for providing all the photographs.

First published in 1973 by Octopus Books Limited, 59 Grosvenor Street, London W1X 9DA.

ISBN 0 7064 0290 1

© 1973 Octopus Books Limited

Book layout by Artes Graphicae Limited, 26 Harrison Street, London WC1

Distributed in Australia by Rigby Limited 30 North Terrace, Kent Town Adelaide, South Australia 5067

Printed in Czechoslovakia

INTRODUCTION

There are a number of reasons which cause people to sew their own garments. A lot of people sew for economy and this particularly applies to mothers of young families who find the price of ready-to-wear children's clothes quite exorbitant and as a result decide to sew their own. Many people, having started with their children's clothes, find that they enjoy creating a garment which is entirely personal and they continue to sew purely for enjoyment, or to provide themselves with the same individuality that they achieved for their children. Quality generally speaks for itself and many women who admire tailored designs are often quite unable to buy such garments off-the-peg owing to their extreme cost. Most of us, in one way or another, have to budget our money but home sewers can use their dress allowances for a length of lovely fabric, for haberdashery requirements and for a pattern coming to the same amount of money. In this way a garment of a much higher standard and quality is achieved. A well-fitting garment of good quality is one of the prime reasons that women sew.

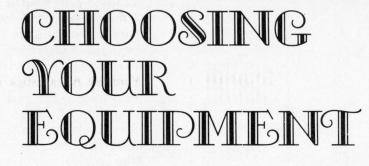

CHOOSING YOUR EQUIPMENT

Once you learn to sew well and quickly, it is likely that you will always sew. For this reason it is a good investment to buy the best quality equipment you can afford. Some tools are essential, whilst others help to make life easier. With such a wealth of sewing aids available to choose from, it is sometimes difficult to distinguish between tools on which money is well spent and those that will not be used often. The following guide lists sewing equipment in two categories.

Basic equipment

Bent handled dressmakers' shears These are the most accurate for cutting fabric because the lower blade rests flat on the cutting surface. The lower ring is round for the thumb and the elongated ring is for the fingers. Left handed models are available. To keep shears in good working order, lubricate the joint of the shears with one drop of oil each month, keep the joint free from lint and fluff and never try to sharpen scissors yourself (diagram 1).

Trimming scissors These are about 6 inches long. They have identical rings for each handle and fairly sharp points. They are used for trimming and clipping seams and should be kept near the machine for clipping threads (diagram 2).

Embroidery scissors Smaller, about 4 inches long, embroidery scissors have very sharp points, and identical rings for each handle. They are useful for cutting threads, clipping seams in fine fabrics and for cutting buttonholes (diagram 3).

Pinking shears Never use pinking shears for cutting out because they cut a zig zag edge which can cause inaccuracy. They are

6

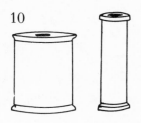

7

8

9

10

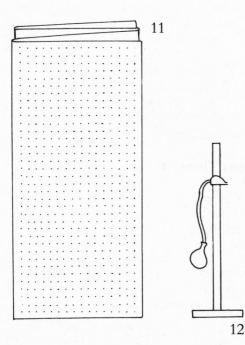

11

12

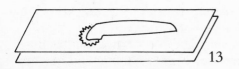

13

excellent however for a quick and easy method of neatening seams and hem edges (diagram 4).

Pins Fine steel pins, 1–1⅜ inches long are best. The brilliantly coloured glass headed pins are very sharp and useful for fitting as they are easy to handle and to see (diagram 5).

Tape measure Usually 60 inches in length, the best tape measures are made of glass fibre and do not tear or stretch. Most measures nowadays are marked in both inches and centimetres (diagram 6).

Yardstick A yardstick is a 36 inch long ruler and is useful for measuring from grainline to selvedge, to ensure the correct placement of pattern pieces and for measuring hems. Choose one with a smooth finish to avoid snagging the fabric. Yardsticks have both Imperial and metric measurements on them (diagram 7).

Thimble One with a steel lining will give the longest wear. It should fit the middle finger of the sewing hand comfortably and although it may seem strange at first, persevere in wearing it. A thimble saves wear and tear on the fingers and time when doing hand sewing (diagram 8).

Needles Hand sewing needles range from size 1 (coarsest) to to size 10 (finest) and come in several types (diagram 9).

Sharps – medium length needles with round eyes for all purpose use.

Betweens – short needles with round eyes for fine sewing.

Millinery – long slender needles with round eyes used for hand basting, gathering and shirring.

Crewel – medium length needles with oblong eyes used for embroidery. As threading them is easy, some dressmakers use these in preference to sharps.

Thread

This should be matched both by colour and fibre to the fabric. If an exact colour match is not available, choose one shade darker (diagram 10).

Mercerized cotton thread is used for all fabrics made from natural fibres such as cotton, linen, silk and wool.

All purpose synthetic threads These can be made of nylon, polyester or cotton covered polyester and are recommended for sewing knitted and synthetic fabrics where elasticity and strength are important.

Silk thread Silk is an alternative thread for sewing natural fibres, particularly silk and is also excellent for basting velvet where other threads might spoil the pile.

Buttonhole Twist This is a strong silk thread, ideal for decorative top stitching. It is also excellent for hand worked buttonholes and for sewing on buttons.

Additional sewing equipment

Cutting Board The floor or the carpet are not good places to cut out. A cutting board, which can be placed on top of a table to enlarge and protect it, is made from heavy cardboard and can be folded up for easy storage (diagram 11).

Skirt marker This is used to measure the distance from the garment hem to the floor. One type uses powdered chalk which is puffed on to the garment and can be operated alone. Another type uses pins but requires the help of a second person (diagram 12).

Tracing wheel Used for marking fabric with dressmaker's carbon paper. Select one with sharp steel points (diagram 13).

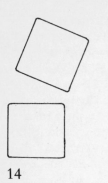

14

15

Dressmaker's carbon paper Used with a tracing wheel for transferring pattern markings on to fabric. Choose a colour close to that of the fabric. When using this method of marking it is important to use only enough pressure on the wheel to make a mark but not enough to show on the right side of the fabric.

Tailor's chalk This is used for marking heavy fabrics such as wool. Two different coloured pieces are needed, one white and one blue. Tailor's chalk is also useful for marking fitting alterations on a garment (diagram 14).

Dressmaker's dummy There are many modern dress stands made of cardboard or wire mesh which can be adjusted to fit personal measurements. Cover with a closely fitting slip or vest. A dummy is useful when lining garments and for tailoring (diagram 15).

Full length mirror For everyone who sews a long mirror is essential. It enables you to study your own figure before deciding on a particular design and is invaluable when fitting a garment for oneself.

Sewing machines

A sewing machine will be the most important of all your sewing tools. Although at this stage, one might be tempted to buy a new modern machine, the older machines were very strongly built. Choose a re-conditioned model and it will continue to do good plain sewing for many years.

If you prefer to buy a new machine there is a variety of different makes available and these fall into four basic categories.

Straight stitch This machine simply sews forwards and backwards in a variety of stitch lengths and is usually sold with some attachments such as a zipper foot. It is always advisable to enquire what attachments are sold with the machine and what further attachments are available separately.

Swing needle In addition to straight stitching, this machine will also do zig-zag stitching. The zig-zag feature is particularly useful for neatening seams, sewing 'knit' fabrics and for creating decorative effects. It is also possible to make button holes with the zig-zag stitch. These machines are usually provided with a good range of attachments and additional attachments can be purchased separately.

Semi-automatic This type of machine is particularly useful because in addition to the zig-zag and straight stitching, it can do from three to six decorative stitches. Step stitch is sometimes one of the range of stitches and this is particularly useful for neatening the edges of fine fabrics. The different stitches included in semi-automatic machines vary from manufacturer to manufacturer and it is important to shop around in order to find out which particular machine will best suit your needs.

Fully-automatic This type of machine is the most expensive to buy but it includes a variety of embroidery stitches in addition to the others already mentioned. Before buying one of these machines, consider how much use the machine will actually get. Bear in mind the fact that to be able to do all these stitches the machine is a very complicated and expensive piece of machinery and unless the embroidery stitches are likely to be used frequently, it will not prove to be a good purchase.

All sewing machines need regular cleaning and oiling, particularly the more elaborate ones. Always read the instruction

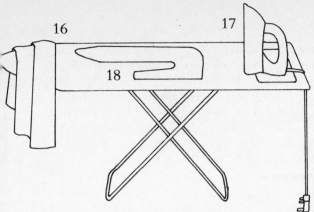

book carefully before using the machine for the first time. Many manufacturers offer sewing demonstrations to prospective purchasers and some dealers will loan you a machine for trial in your own home for a few days. This will give you a chance to try it on various types of fabrics.

It is very important to have the machine threaded up properly with the bobbin correctly inserted. If, even after reading the instruction booklet, you are in any doubt as to how this should be done, contact your dealer for further instruction.

The correct needle size is also important and the instruction book will tell you what size is suitable for the fabric you are working on. Man-made fibres tend to blunt needles faster than natural fibres and it is possible that after you have sewn a complete garment in a man-made fabric, the machine needle will be blunt. Use a fresh needle for each new sewing job. Obtaining the correct stitch size and tension is important in good sewing. Most modern machines are adjusted so that all but the very finest or the very heaviest fabrics can be sewn on a standard tension. On a perfect seam the stitches should look the same on both sides. A stitch length of 12 to 15 stitches per inch is usually satisfactory for fine to medium weight fabrics. Heavy weight fabrics and heavy furnishing fabrics, and some special fabrics such as velvet, will require a stitch length of approximately 10 to 12 stitches per inch.

Before stitching the seam on the actual garment, always test the thread, tension and stitch length on fabric scraps first of all. If the tension is not right, instructions for adjusting this will be given in the sewing machine instruction booklet.

Pressing equipment

Whilst no one piece of dressmaking equipment is going to revolutionize your life, without using your pressing equipment you will never achieve a successful garment. Always remember, you make half of your garment with your iron. Keep your pressing equipment near your sewing machine and then it is no problem to press as you go.

An ironing board should adjust to different heights, be well padded and have a well-secured cotton cover (diagram 16).

An iron is needed for pressing open seams as you work as well as for pressing at finished stages. A steam and dry iron combined is the most useful. Make sure the base plate is not scratched and always keep it clean (diagram 17).

A sleeve board is sometimes supplied with the ironing board, or it can be purchased separately. This too should be well padded and cotton covered. A sleeve board enables you to press sleeve seams open and other areas which are difficult to reach (diagram 18).

A pressing cloth is used to prevent fabric from getting a shine. Muslin is good for most purposes. A piece of the same fabric is best for pressing wool fabrics.

A pounding block is a wooden clapper which is used when a seam needs firm treatment. The seam is first steam pressed then after the iron and press cloth have been removed, the block is clapped down on the fabric to flatten the seam (diagram 19).

A Seam roll is used to prevent seam turnings showing through to the right side of the garment after it has been pressed. If you press seams open over this, the iron only comes in contact with the line of stitching (diagram 20).

9

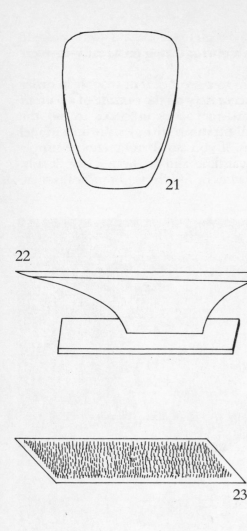

21

22

23

A *tailor's ham* is a firmly stuffed cushion shaped like a ham used to press darts and curved seams to give a soft shaping (diagram 21).

A *point presser* is used to press collars, corners and facings, where a sharp point is required (diagram 22).

A *velvet board* is used to press velvet, corduroy and other pile fabrics. The fabric is placed right side down on to the needles to prevent the pile being flattened during pressing (diagram 23).

The value of pressing can never be over-emphasized and the motto is 'stitch then press'. This does not mean that you must spend your time jumping up from your machine after having stitched a dart, to press it, and then having to go back and repeat the performance. A good way of working is to stitch the darts in the front and back of a skirt for instance and then the centre back seam. You then have one seam and at least four darts to press at one time.

Every line of stitching *must* be pressed before the section is joined to another part of the garment.

Pressing is quite different from ironing. With ironing, a hot iron is smoothed across fabric to remove creases. With pressing, a press cloth is placed over the fabric and the iron pressed down firmly on to the area and then lifted.

Working with a dry iron The iron should be set to cotton and the press cloth moistened with water and then wrung out thoroughly. The cloth is then placed over the fabric. The iron is applied firmly.

Working with a steam iron Many fabrics can be pressed from the wrong side without a press cloth. As a general rule, the heavier the fabric the more steam is required to press it. Therefore, very heavy tweeds will require a wool press cloth, medium weight cloths may not need one at all.

Removing shine Apply a solution of white vinegar with a sponge to the affected area, and then press using a press cloth. Then brush the fabric with a clothes brush. An alternative method is to lay the press cloth over the fabric and hold an iron approximately $\frac{1}{2}$ inch away, and move it continually but very slowly so that the steam penetrates the fabric. These methods can also be applied to remove creases from garments when making alterations.

Special fabrics Pile fabrics, such as velvet and corduroy, should always be pressed on a velvet board. Knitted fabrics should always be pressed with a gentle stamping motion along the lengthwise ribs, and not ironed across them as this will cause the ribs to stretch. Lace should be placed face down over a wool press cloth or a thick towel and pressed on the wrong side using a muslin press cloth.

Making the most of yourself

When you buy ready-to-wear clothes from a shop, you probably take three or four different designs into a changing room to try them on to see which particular design suits your figure type best. The same rules apply to home dressmaking.

First of all take a good long look at yourself in front of a mirror wearing very little clothing such as basic underwear, or a bathing suit. It is most important at this stage to be honest with yourself and decide whether your figure is of a curvy nature or if you have a very short back or short legs. It is then up to you to apply the rules of basic good dress sense to your own figure when choosing a design to sew, just as you would do when looking at yourself in a mirror trying on a ready-to-wear garment.

Pattern manufacturers go to a great deal of trouble in order to represent each garment accurately on the outside of a pattern envelope and in their catalogue pages in order to aid the customer. However, these illustrations are normally on a model of perfect body proportions. If you lack height, choose simple designs unbroken at the waistline and without fussy details. Avoid boxy outlines, wide hems or full sleeves or ruffles as these add width.

Shirts and trousers for men

11

Fabric used to suit a style

Details such as collars and pockets create design interest and should not be placed at a point where emphasis is not required. Keep the figure balanced by creating distracting interest – on the bodice for instance if you are heavy hipped, or at the hipline if you have heavy shoulders. If the hips are narrow, pockets at this level will balance the figure well.

For all except the very thin, a princess line dress is a useful design to start with as it can be trimmed to suit individual figure types and at the same time provides sufficient seams to enable the garment to be fitted successfully. One last piece of advice: do not attempt a design which is beyond your sewing capabilities. Commercial patterns indicate those designs which are easy to sew and by choosing a superb fabric, you can make a simply designed garment look wonderful.

Before actually beginning a fabric hunt, purchase the paper pattern first. The back of a pattern envelope quotes the amount of fabric required for the design, and gives this in different fabric widths. If you have already bought a length of fabric, you could find you have either too much or not enough and thus have to change your mind and start on a new design altogether. A beginner is often tempted to select a very cheap fabric for her first dressmaking attempt to avoid wastage, should the garment not turn out as she expected. This, however, usually turns out to be false economy as very cheap fabrics hardly ever do justice to even the very best hand work. Obviously it would be foolhardy to go for the most expensive fabric, you would be well advised to select a cloth of medium quality and particularly one which presses well. Checked and striped fabrics should be avoided for a first attempt in dressmaking and one-way fabrics such as velvet and corduroy which have a 'nap' should also be left until you are more experienced. Very good quality cotton with plenty of body will provide an economical starting point and in addition you will not experience difficulties making up this fabric. The easiest choice for a first effort is a woollen material which will handle beautifully although this may be more expensive. Commercial paper patterns supply fabric suggestions on the back of the pattern envelope and although these notes tend to be vague they do give you an excellent guide as to the weight of fabric which will respond well to the design illustrated. Some designs are planned specifically for 'knits only' and in these instances a guide to the weight of fabric is also quoted. Sometimes the pattern gives an indication as to how much elasticity the knitted fabric should contain. Fabrics should always be tested for their crease resistance and it is always well worth enquiring as to the fibre content of the fabric and whether it will wash, or has to be dry cleaned.

The colour of fabric which you select to use, whether a printed fabric or a plain cloth, remains your individual choice. Bear in mind your hair colour and your skin colour when making your choice and remember that darker colours tend to reduce your apparent size. Conversely, brighter colours tend to make you look larger. Most shops will allow you to remove a roll of fabric from the rack and drape it over one shoulder so that you can see the effect of the colour when worn by you. In addition, it will enable you to assess the draping qualities of the fabric. If at this point the fabric does not hang smoothly when you gather it up in your hand, you can be sure that it is quite unsuitable for a design featuring gathers.

Before purchasing a length of fabric check that it has no flaws and confirm the width of the fabric with the sales assistant. And make one final check with the yardage on the back of the pattern envelope to make sure that you have asked for the correct amount of fabric, before it is cut off.

Haberdashery and notions

It is infuriating to find that you are missing a particular item when you are all set to start sewing, so whilst you are in the shop, choose thread, zips, buttons and other notions listed on the back of the pattern envelope. This usually lists haberdashery requirements under each particular garment. For instance, if the pattern is of a wardrobe variety containing pattern pieces for a skirt, jacket, trousers and blouse, make sure that you have bought the buttons for the jacket as well as for the blouse. A little time spent at this stage, will save a lot of time wasted later on.

An excellent range of buttons is available in most shops, but if you should experience difficulty in finding a good match to your fabric, some stores will cover buttons for you or you can purchase button moulds to enable you to cover your own.

Zip fasteners are available in a wide range of colours and in different weights. The zip fastener pack usually carries a guide as to the suitability of the zip weight and gives insertion instructions. It is particularly important to ensure that the zip is strong enough to stand up to the strain it will take, but at the same time it must not be too bulky thus creating a bump. Open ended zips for cardigans and jackets and curved zips for trouser front fastenings are available. Plastic zips in decorative colours make a point of emphasis at the front of a dress or jacket.

Thread, elastic, bias seam binding, hooks and eyes and snap fasteners should all be purchased when you buy the fabric.

Interfacings and linings

Interfacing may be necessary for the pattern and will be quoted as a requirement on the back of the pattern envelope if it is needed. Interfacing is used to reinforce areas such as the front facing of a blouse where button holes are to be worked, and for stiffening collars and cuffs. Woven interfacing has a grain and pattern pieces should be pinned on to it with the grain in the same direction as for the top fabric. Non-woven interfacing has no grain and may be cut in any direction. Each year, a larger variety of non-woven interfacings becomes available and manufacturers produce booklets to guide the consumer in choosing the correct weight which should be used. Iron-on interfacing is available in either woven or non-woven varieties and instead of being applied to the inside of the garment is usually ironed on to the facings. When purchasing interfacing, it is a good idea to match the care properties of the interfacing to the fabric so that washable fabrics contain a washable interfacing. For tailored garments such as a jacket or coat it is usually advisable to use a linen or hair canvas interfacing. Special collar canvas can be purchased for pad stitching inside collars but if you are in doubt as to what weight to buy, go to a large store and consult an experienced assistant.

Lining may also be necessary to complete your garment and the yardage of this will be indicated on the back of the pattern envelope if it is required. If a pattern suggests an underlining, do not become confused and search frantically for an underlining. This is simply a method of construction which is explained on page 109. An underlining fabric should be chosen carefully to give fabric more body so that it holds its shape and hangs well. This type of lining is often used for a sculptured design with simple seaming detail.

Lining gives a professional finish to the inside of a garment and prevents the garment from coming into direct contact with the body. This ensures that the garment hangs well because the lining fabric slips easily over areas where the somewhat rougher top fabric might tend to catch or cling. A loose lining will also help to prevent creasing and seating but greater protection against these will be achieved by underlining your garment. Common lining fabrics are rayon taffeta, tricel taffeta or jap silk. Tricel taffeta is suitable for most washable medium weight fabrics but if you wish to line a light weight fabric try to obtain washable jap silk. Rayon taffeta is suitable for medium and heavy weight fabrics which need to be dry cleaned. A satin lining of slightly heavier weight is normally used for jackets and coats. Refer to the linings chart for further information.

Suitable linings for different fabric weights

Garment fabric	Underlining	Interfacing	Lining
See-through fabrics	Organdie or pure silk organza	For silk use pure silk organza. Organdie or very light-weight non-woven	Jap silk and light weight rayon or Tricel taffeta
Lightweight cotton, silk, rayon, linen and wool	Soft cotton lawn or lightweight rayon	Iron-on or non-woven as recommended by the manufacturer	Jap silk and rayon and Tricel taffeta
Medium weight cotton, rayon, linen, silk and wool	Soft cotton lawn or medium weight rayon	Pre-shrunk cotton or iron-on or non-woven as recommended by the manufacturer	Tricel taffeta or jap silk
Man made fibres	Rayon	Non-woven interfacing as recommended by the manufacturer	Tricel taffeta

Paper patterns

Commercial paper patterns probably constitute the most important aid to successful home dressmaking.

You may find that one particular brand of commercial pattern fits you better than another and will therefore require less alteration. You may also get used to following the instructions given by a particular company. All the major paper pattern companies base their designs on the same set of standard body measurements but if you find a particular make which supplies you with the fashion you like and a good fit, you are well advised to continue using that make. A very cheap pattern must inevitably give you less, either in terms of instruction or design, and is not recommened for beginners. With a particularly expensive pattern you are probably paying extra because it is a design original and therefore more costly to produce.

The amount of fit in a garment is always a matter of personal taste and all patterns are cut with a tolerance or ease to allow for comfortable wearability and movement. The amount of ease allowed varies betwen garments such as a closely fitting evening dress and a coat which has a lining and is to be worn over other garments.

The envelope front

The front of a pattern envelope displays the manufacturer's name and the pattern number, together with the price. The various design views will be illustrated, usually in suitable fabrics and each view is numbered. The sizing group will be quoted (i.e. Miss, or Miss Petite), together with the size (i.e. Size 12 Bust 34). When you open the pattern envelope to remove the pattern tissue, it is advisable to check and see that the tissue pattern pieces are printed with the same size as that which is quoted on the outside of the pattern envelope. The envelope may also indicate that the pattern is easy to sew, or designed for knit fabrics only. Always ensure that you fully understand the meaning of this information and if you are in any doubt at all, ask the sales assistant for advice. On the back of the pattern envelope is a wealth of information which is very easy to understand once you are used to the format.

The envelope back

Pattern description This will give you detailed information about the various views to clarify the design on the front of the pattern envelope and will state where trims have been added.

Back view drawings will enable you to see whether the skirt has pleats in the back as well as the front.

Pattern pieces are accurately scaled down and illustrated with each piece clearly marked. You will be able to see how much shaping is included in the centre back or side seams or how much fullness is included in a sleeve.

Suggested fabrics are always included. If the list is general, all fabrics will be suitable for all views. However, check right through to ensure that the fabric for one view is not different from the others.

Garment title lists the actual garments which are included in the pattern.

Extra fabric suggestions are included inside the yardage box and usually say which fabrics are not suitable for the particular design.

Standard body measurements are shown on the back of the envelope for easy reference. These represent your body measurements and not those of the finished garment.

The yardage box will show how much fabric is required for each view in a variety of fabric widths. It will also quote yardages for trimmings, lining and interlining.

Garment measurements such as the finished back length or the width at the lower edge of a garment are quoted here. If you are unsure, check these against an existing garment to see if any adjustments are necessary.

Sewing notions such as zips, buttons, thread, hooks and eyes, snap fasteners and seam bindings, etc., are listed in quantity as well as size.

The number of pattern pieces included in the pattern is also given and will indicate to a limited extent how easy or difficult the garment is to sew.

It is always advisable to put a pencil ring round the view you propose to make on the front of the pattern envelope. On the back of the envelope, this view can be clearly underlined.

A simple A-line style for a long skirt

Thereafter, after you have determined which pattern size to use, you can quickly determine how much fabric you will require in a certain width. At the same time mark your interfacing and lining requirements with a ring and underline such sewing notions as you require. This will enable you quickly and easily to purchase all your requirements in one shop at one time.

Inside the pattern envelope

The instruction sheet Generally, beginners pay insufficient attention to the instruction sheet inside the envelope. By following it closely, all sewing processes are quickly and easily undertaken. Line drawings for each view are included and pattern pieces are identified by number and name. How many pattern pieces you require for each view is clearly marked and which pattern pieces these are. As you select your paper pattern pieces, it is advisable to return those which you will not require to the pattern envelope and check against this list to ensure you have all the pattern pieces which you will need. Another section explains the pattern markings, i.e., notches, cutting line, stitching line, and lengthening and shortening lines. It will also give instructions for laying out the pattern pieces on to the fabric, saying when a pattern piece should be placed with the printed side up and when it should be placed with the printed side down; how to cope with nap or one-way fabrics, and how to cope with a pattern piece if it is depicted in the cutting layouts as extending over the fold of a fabric. For instance, the pattern piece may be illustrated with the printed side of the pattern uppermost. All surrounding pattern pieces which are normally cut through double thickness should be cut out and then the fabric is opened up to single thickness and the pattern piece placed on the fabric printed side uppermost and cut out. Further important cutting notes may be found at the beginning of the cutting layouts or alternatively at the beginning of a particular view in the cutting layouts.

Sewing directions are found on the reverse side of the instruction sheet and take the dressmaker through the making up of the garment step by step. Scale diagrams depict most processes but it is important to read the accompanying text. The wording is always as simple as possible without leaving out important points.

1	Casual ensemble for weekend wear
2,3	Sewing doll
4	Ruffles by night
5	Sew for the man in your life too
6	Purchased ruffles add glamour to a blouse
7	Patch pockets use stripes on the crosswise grain
8	Shirts in stripes mix and match
9	Superb appliqué
10	Sewing for children is such fun
11	Sewing for a bed-sitter
12	A place setting
13	Mix and match table cloths
14	Wardrobe accessories
15	Baby's pillow case and blanket

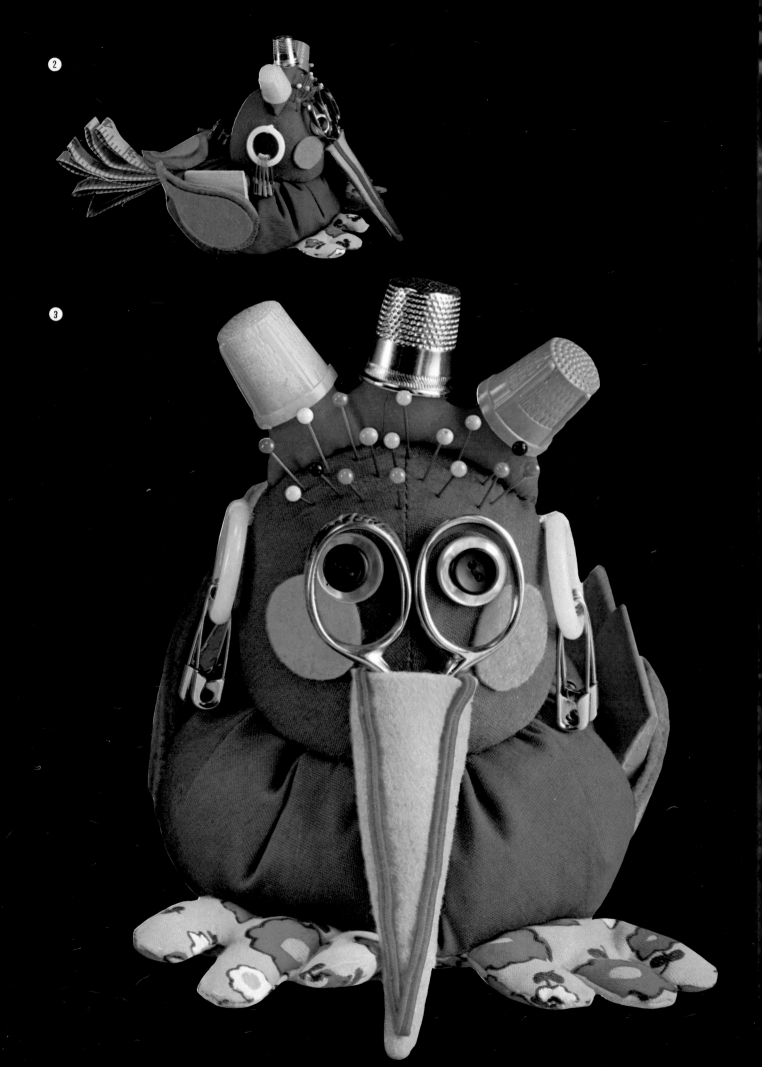

BEGINNING TO SEW

A perfect fit

The fault	Fault identification	Garment remedy	Pattern alteration

Full neck Neckline is too tight and wrinkles occur immediately below. Clip into seam allowance until tightness eases and garment lies flat. Mark new neckline at base of clips and seam line $\frac{5}{8}$ inch from this.

On neck edge of pattern mark a new seamline with seam line $\frac{5}{8}$ inch from this. Make same adjustment on neck facing.

Sloping shoulders Extra fullness will show at the shoulder with some lower down armhole. Shoulder seam can be lifted at outer edges. Snip into seam allowance at underarm and lower by an equal amount.

On pattern mark new shoulder line lowering underarm by an equal amount and draw new armhole curve.

Square shoulders Fabric will strain at armhole end of shoulder seam. Undo shoulder seam, reduce seam turning at armhole edge and increase turning at neck edge.

On pattern mark new shoulder line and raise underarm by an equal amount drawing in the new armhole curve.

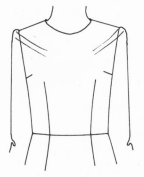

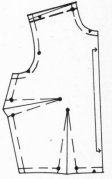

Broad shoulders Garment will pull across top of sleeves, chest and back. Remove the sleeves and repin in position reducing seam turning by up to $\frac{3}{8}$ inch on the front and back bodice.

On front and back bodice pattern pieces draw a line 5–6 inches long from centre of shoulder line down into the bodice. Connect to armhole seam line with horizontal line. Cut pattern on this line and spread the requisite amount. Draw new cutting line between neckline and armhole.

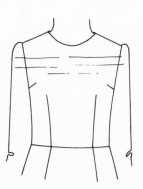

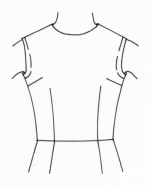

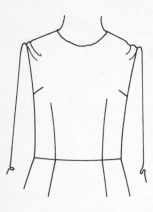

Narrow shoulders Sleeve seams will fall over shoulders. Remove sleeve from armhole and refit taking larger seam turning from the bodice. Draw a line 5–6 inches long from the centre of the shoulder seam and connect to armhole seam with a horizontal line.

Cut the pattern on this line and overlap the edges to reduce the shoulder length. Draw a new shoulder line from neckline to armhole edge.

Tight armholes Armholes are too tight and wrinkles occur. Clip into seam allowance until tightness eases and garment lies flat. Mark new armhole at base of clips and seamline $\frac{5}{8}$ inch from this.

On front and back bodice pattern pieces lower armhole at the side seam and draw a new armhole curve from this to the point of shoulder. If excessive adjustment is made, the sleeve head may also need to be adjusted.

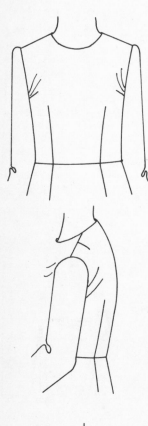

Rounded shoulders Fullness will appear at the back armholes and the back bodice will pull at the waistline. Reduce seam turning by up to $\frac{3}{8}$ inch at the back waistline tapering off towards the side seams. Seam turning may also be reduced at neckline. Increase shoulder darts by up to $\frac{3}{8}$ inch which is taken from armhole seam turnings. Repin shoulder seams remembering that armhole turnings are reduced.

On back pattern piece draw a line across to centre of armhole seamline and slash. Separate edges by the requisite amount and pin to paper. Draw a new cutting line from the lower part of bodice straight up to form new centre back seam. Straighten curve of neckline. Shorten shoulder dart and add back neck dart to take out the amount added by the new centre back seam. If pattern has neck dart already, simply widen the dart by the necessary amount.

Erect back Fullness occurs at the centre back in the shoulder area. Increase seam turnings at centre back of neck line tapering off to the shoulder and increase turnings at centre back of waist line again tapering to the side seam.

On back pattern piece draw a straight line from centre back to centre of armhole seam line and slash. Overlap the edges and pin in position. Straighten centre back seam as shown reduce dart by the same amount as you removed from the centre back seam. This dart may be omitted altogether.

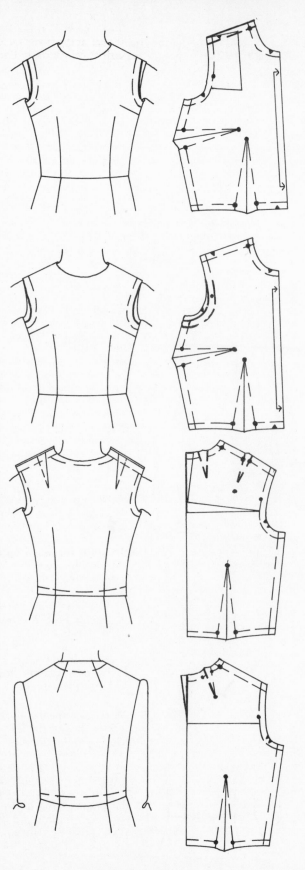

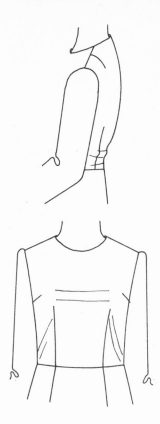

Sway back Wrinkles and excess fabric appear at the waistline of both bodice and skirt at centre back. Undo waist seam and repin taking extra seam turning to accommodate excess fabric from bodice and skirt. Darts may need refitting.

On back bodice pattern piece reduce back waist length by requisite amount and taper off to side seam. A similar adjustment should be made to the skirt pattern pieces.

Full bust Tightness will be evident across the bust and the waist could rise at side seams. Undo side seams and pin up to $\frac{3}{8}$ inch from waist seam into underarm bust dart. Up to $\frac{3}{8}$ inch may also be added into waist line dart from side seam. Repin side seams remembering that seam turnings are now reduced.

On front bodice pattern piece draw a straight line from the centre of underarm bust dart to centre front and another from centre of waistline dart to shoulder seam line. Slash, place over tissue paper and spread the pattern pieces as indicated by half the amount required. If pattern has only one dart such as french dart, continue slash line of dart to centre front seam. Place pattern over tissue, slash from side seam through dart to centre front seam and spread the pattern by half the amount needed at the point of bust. Pin to tissue and redraw dart.

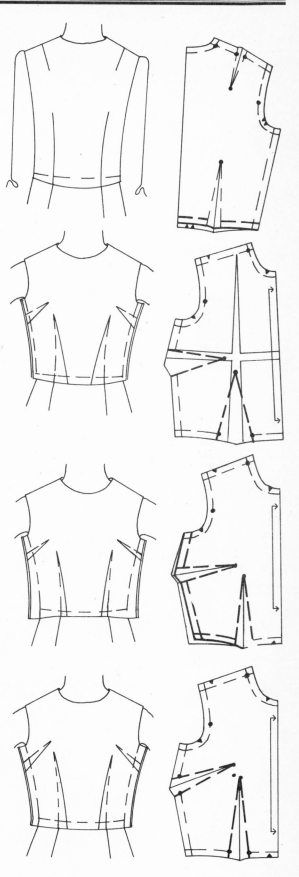

Small bust The point of underarm bust darts create fullness over the bust. Undo side seams and let out side bust dart on the lower stitching line. This will increase the seam turning into the waist. It may also be necessary to let out waist line darts taking excess fabric into the side seams.

On front bodice pattern piece reduce underarm bust dart and waist line dart. Raise cutting line for waist at the side seam by the equivalent amount and decrease lower edge of side seam also. Draw new cutting lines to centre front and armhole edges.

High bust Bust darts are too low creating fullness below the bust and tightness occurs over the point of the bust. Pin the correct position for the point of bust and undo darts. Darts should be repinned towards the new point of bust.

On front of bodice pattern piece raise the point of the underarm bust dart by requisite amount and draw in new lines. Raise point of waist line dart by the same amount and draw in new lines.

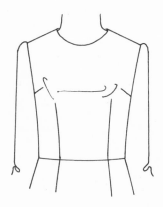

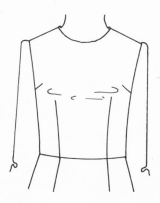

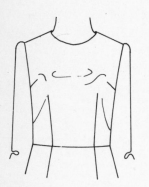

Low bust Fullness occurs above bust and fabric pulls over bust itself. Pin correct position for point of bust and undo darts. Repin towards the point of bust.

On front bodice pattern lower point of bust for underarm bust dart and redraw dart. Lower point of waistline dart the same amount and redraw dart.

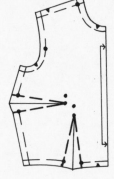

Small waist Fullness and extra fabric occurs at the waistline. Increase darts and take in side seams.

On front and back pattern pieces for both bodice and skirt waistline darts should be increased and cutting lines at side seams tapered in. Redraw darts and new seam lines.

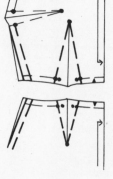

Large waist Tightness at waist with wrinkles above and below. Undo waist seam, decrease darts and let out side seams.

On front and back pattern pieces for bodice and skirt decrease the size of waistline darts and draw in new side seams having extra width at this point. Draw in new darts and seam line.

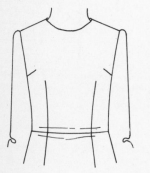

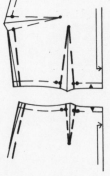

Large hips Tightness which causes wrinkling will be evident at hip level. Let out side seams and reduce turnings by up to $\frac{3}{8}$ inch through to waistline. Increase waist darts to bring waistline back to original size.

On front and back skirt pattern pieces add a quarter of the amount needed to the four side seams from waist to hem level. Increase the dart by the same amount to restore waistline to its original size.

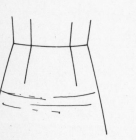
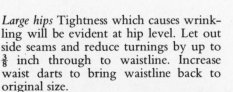

High hips Skirt will appear shorter on one side and centre line of skirt will not hang straight. Release up to ⅜ inch from the waistline turnings on the high hip side into skirt. Restitch waistline seam remembering that turnings are now reduced.

On back and front skirt pattern pieces draw a vertical line through the centre of the dart to the point and from there take the line horizontally out to the side seam. Slash from side seam to point of dart and raise the upper part by the amount needed. This will automatically decrease the dart. Slash through dart and pin pattern pieces flat. This alteration must be effected for one side only, left or right. Effect alteration on duplicate pattern piece cut from tissue and then attach to original pattern piece. Pattern piece will now cut one whole front and one whole back so fabric should be cut on single thickness.

Thin arms Sleeves appear generally baggy at upper and lower arms. Remove sleeve from armhole at underarm and take in underarm seam throughout its length. It may also be necessary to take in the side seam at the underarm slightly.

On sleeve pattern piece draw a vertical line parallel to the grain line from dot at the centre of the sleeve head through to the hem. On this line make a tuck of the amount needed and pin. Redraw sleeve head to maintain a smooth curve. On the front and back bodice pattern pieces take off half the amount of the tuck from the side seams at the underarm. Taper this amount to nothing at waistline and redraw seam line.

Large arms Tightness across upper and lower arms without sufficient room to move arm freely. Remove sleeve from armhole at underarm and reduce seam turning by up to ⅜ inch throughout its length.

On sleeve pattern piece draw a vertical line parallel to the grain line from dot at the centre of the sleeve head through to the hem. Slash through this line and spread the pattern pieces over tissue by an equal amount throughout. Pin in position and draw new sleeve head. On front and back bodice pattern pieces increase the armhole at the side seam by adding half the amount which was added to the sleeve and taper the side seam to waistline. Draw in new seam line.

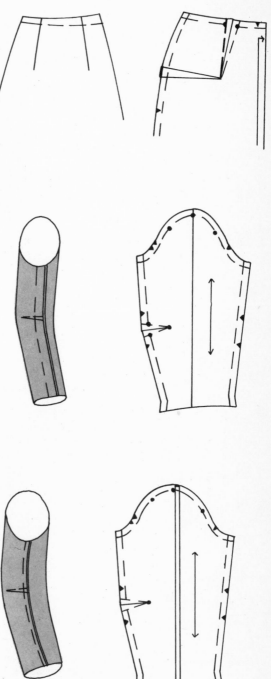

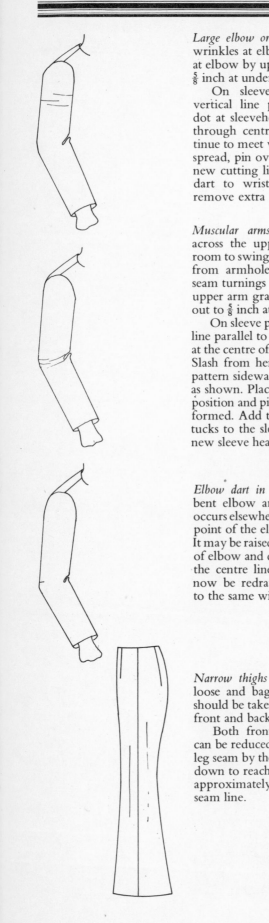

Large elbow or upper arms Tightness and wrinkles at elbow. Reduce seam turning at elbow by up to $\frac{3}{8}$ inch tapering back to $\frac{5}{8}$ inch at underarm and wrist.

On sleeve pattern piece, draw a vertical line parallel to grainline from dot at sleevehead to elbow. Draw a line through centre of elbow dart and continue to meet vertical line. Slash open and spread, pin over tissue paper and draw in new cutting line from upper cut edge of dart to wrist. Increase elbow dart to remove extra length added to seamline.

Muscular arms Tightness and drawing across the upper arm without sifficient room to swing arm freely. Remove sleeve from armhole at underarm and reduce seam turnings of sleeve by up to $\frac{3}{8}$ inch at upper arm graduating seam turning back out to $\frac{5}{8}$ inch at lower edge.

On sleeve pattern piece draw a vertical line parallel to the grain line from the dot at the centre of the sleeve head to the hem. Slash from hem to seam line spread the pattern sideways by the required amount as shown. Place pattern over tissue pin in position and pin out the tucks which have formed. Add the amount included in the tucks to the sleeve head and draw in the new sleeve head.

Elbow dart in wrong place When arm is bent elbow area feels tight and fullness occurs elsewhere. The dart should be at the point of the elbow when the arm is bent. It may be raised or lowered. Mark position of elbow and draw in new line parallel to the centre line of old dart. Dart should now be redrawn either side of this line to the same width as the old one.

Narrow thighs Trousers will appear too loose and baggy at the thigh. Garment should be taken in on inner leg seam both front and back.

Both front and back pattern pieces can be reduced at the crutch on the inside leg seam by the required amount tapering down to reach the original cutting line at approximately knee level. Draw in new seam line.

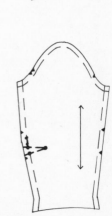

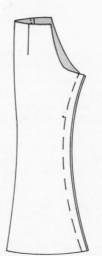

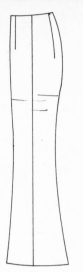

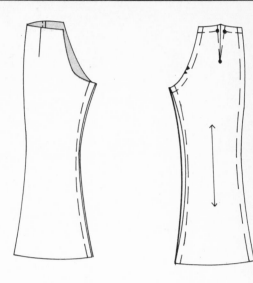

Heavy thighs Trousers will be tight across the thighs and wrinkle. Inside leg seams of trouser can be reduced by up to $\frac{3}{8}$ inch and if necessary outside leg seams can be reduced also. Seam turning should be graduated back out to $\frac{5}{8}$ inch by knee level.

On front and back trouser pattern pieces a new inside leg seam is cut as indicated adding the required amount. If necessary the same adjustment may be carried out on side seams. Draw in new seam lines.

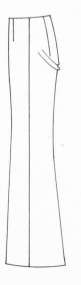

Large bottom Trousers will pull across the back drawing side seams towards the back. Reduce centre back seam by up to $\frac{3}{8}$ inch. Back side seam may also be reduced if necessary. Increase darts to restore waistline to its original size. On back pattern piece slash along lengthening and shortening lines from centre back to side seamline. Place over tissue paper, spread the required amount and pin. Draw in new centre back seam and increase darts to bring waistline back to original size.

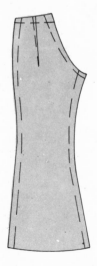

Small bottom Trousers will bag over the buttocks and wrinkles will appear across the seat at hip level. Increase waist line seam turning at centre back tapering off to $\frac{5}{8}$ inch at side seam. Dart should be made smaller and extra fabric taken out at the centre back seam.

On back pattern piece take a diagonal tuck in the centre back seam tapering out to the side seam. Pin in position and redraw the centre back crutch seam.

Large abdomen Reduce seam turning at centre of waist line by up to $\frac{3}{8}$ inch graduating back to $\frac{5}{8}$ inch at side seam. On front of trousers seam turnings can be reduced by up to $\frac{3}{8}$ inch at centre front crutch seam and side seam. Dart should be increased to reduce waist line to original measurement.

On front pattern piece slash from centre front to side seam, place over tissue paper and spread the required amount. Draw in new centre front seam and increase darts to bring waistline back to original size.

A to Z of sewing terms

Arrow Small arrows on seam lines indicate the direction in which the garment should be cut out and sewn together. Follow arrows to prevent unnecessary stretching. Heavy black arrows found in the centre of the pattern piece indicate the straight of grain.

Basting or tacking Basting is a temporary marking which will hold two or more pieces of fabric together or transfer pattern markings on to fabric. This may be done by hand or machine and, in some circumstances, with pins.

Bias Fold a square piece of fabric in half diagonally and cut along fold. This cut edge forms the true bias.

Bias binding is used for neatening raw edges such as hems or seams and may be purchased. To make your own, stitch together strips of true bias.

Bodice Pattern pieces may be labelled Bodice Front or Bodice Back and the term is given to that part of the garment which runs from shoulder to waist level.

Button holes Hand worked, machined and bound are the three types of button holes. Placement for button holes will always be clearly indicated on the pattern tissue.

Centre back and front This may be indicated by a seam but if pattern piece has been placed to the fold for cutting out, always insert a line of basting to indicate the centre back.

Clip Curved seams are clipped so that they lie flat after pressing. Make small clips into seam allowance almost up to stitching line where seam allowance is on inner curve. If seam allowance is on outer curve, cut out small V shaped pieces of fabric at regular intervals and remove.

Cutting layout The instruction sheet will feature cutting layouts for all views in the same fabric widths which are quoted on the back of the pattern envelope. The illustration will show how to lay pattern pieces out in an economical manner.

Cutting line Refer to key on instruction sheet to check this symbol. It is usually a heavy dark line, broken only by notches, running outermost round each pattern piece. Cut through the centre of the cutting line.

Dart A fold of fabric tapering to a point at one or both ends, usually indicated by broken stitching lines round a solid centre line.

Ease Tolerance may be another word for ease when it means the extra room which is built into a garment to allow for comfortable wearability. Alternatively the word ease is sometimes marked on to pattern pieces to indicate that when a seam is formed, that side of the garment should be eased on to the other because it is slightly longer.

Edge stitching A line of stitching formed approximately $\frac{1}{8}$ inch from a folded or seamed edge.

Envelope The envelope contains the pattern tissue, and the instruction sheet. The front shows illustrations of the various views and the back illustrates back views and quotes the yardages for fabric, lining and interfacing and indicates the sewing notions required.

Fabric widths It is not always possible for a manufacturer to quote yardages for each view in every fabric width available because there are so many available. Popular fabric widths are 36 inch, 45 inch, 54 inch, 60 inch and 70 inch.

Facing A piece of fabric to finish an edge such as an armhole or neck.

Fibres All fabrics are made from a fibre. This may be natural such as cotton, linen, silk and wool or man-made such as polyester, acrylic, nylon, acetate and triacetate. Each fibre is formed into a yarn and the yarn into a fabric.

Figure type Patterns are produced in very wide range of shapes and sizes, each called a figure type. Check your body measurements and use your nearest figure type and size to avoid unnecessary alterations in making up.

Fold A cutting layout will sometimes indicate that the fabric should be placed to the fold. Fabric is usually folded right sides to the inside. A fold line may also be indicated on a pattern.

Gather Gathering is used to draw up fabric on a line of stitching and may be done by machine or hand. The pattern piece will usually indicate where gathering is necessary.

Grain The lengthwise grain of a piece of fabric is depicted by the threads which run parallel to the selvedge. The crosswise grain is indicated by the threads which run across the fabric at 90° to the lengthwise grain.

Grainline This is the lengthwise grain which should match up with the straight of grain on the pattern piece.

Hem An amount of fabric turned up at the lower edge of all garments which is held in place with a hemming stitch.

Hem line The line from which the extra fabric is turned up to form the hem.

Hem allowance This should be indicated at the bottom of each pattern piece and will tell you how deep the hem will be.

Interfacing This is a layer of fabric which is placed between facing and garment on the wrong side to provide extra strength or shaping.

Instruction sheet Follow this carefully for detailed instructions for cutting out and making up your garment.

Layering A method of trimming seam allowances which will remove bulk. Seam allowances are trimmed down to different widths, for instance, one to $\frac{1}{8}$ inch wide and the other to $\frac{1}{4}$ inch wide.

Lengthening and shortening line Usually indicated by double lines. These indicate where the pattern can be adjusted to lengthen or shorten prior to cutting out. Lengthening and shortening lines found on the bodice or above the waist on a dress pattern piece are used only to correct the difference between your own back waist length and that which is quoted for your size on the pattern.

Lining Cut out from the same basic pattern pieces, a lining is usually constructed separately and used to finish off the inside of the garment.

Margin Excess tissue on pattern pieces found outside the cutting lines is referred to as margin. This should never be trimmed away. It is left there on purpose to enable you to cut through the centre of the cutting line to ensure accuracy.

Mark Transfer pattern markings from the pattern on to the fabric. This may be done with dressmakers' carbon paper, tailor's tacks, or tailor's chalk.

Mitre To make neat square corners on fabric or trim, form a diagonal seam from the point of the corner to the inside edge.

Nap Fabrics such as velvet, corduroy and those with a hairy surface are known as napped or pile fabrics. They require a special cutting layout entitled 'with nap' to ensure that all pattern pieces run in the same direction.

Notch Markings, usually a black diamond shape, which should be matched when seams are joined. Always cut notches outwards into the margin.

Notes These are special directions which may be found under the sewing directions or in the cutting layouts which denote points to which special attention should be paid.

Notions Items such as zips, buttons, hooks and eyes and snap fasteners are listed under notions, and indicate what quantity is required and in which size.

Pink To neaten an edge by cutting with pinking shears.

Pleat This may be a small fold of fabric which is not stitched down, or larger such as that found in a skirt. The pattern tissue will indicate by means of solid and broken lines how to fold the fabric and thus form the pleat.

Pattern piece The piece of tissue printed with pattern markings.

Ravel Ravel means fray.

Reinforce It is often necessary to strengthen or reinforce the inside corner of a piece of fabric prior to attaching other pieces to it. The corner is stay stitched $\frac{5}{8}$ inch from the raw edge, and then the fabric clipped from the raw edge up to the corner stay stitching.

Right side All pattern manufacturers indicate in the key on the instruction sheet how they will depict the right side of the fabric.

Seam line This line is usually $\frac{5}{8}$ inch from the cut edge; when two pieces of fabric are sewn together along this line, a seam is formed.

Seam allowance This is normally $\frac{5}{8}$ inch, except in special circumstances where the seam allowance would be clearly marked otherwise.

Simple pleats for a 1920s look

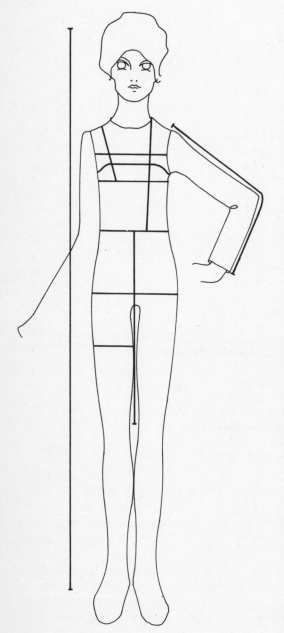

Selvedge The woven edge which runs down both sides of a piece of fabric is termed the selvedge.

Shank Buttons sewn on to suits and coats and heavier garments need to have a space left between the button and the fabric known as the shank.

Shortening lines See lengthening and shortening lines.

Slash To cut open. The term is often applied to darts which are cut open to flatten them, and also to pattern pieces when pattern alterations are made.

Stay stitch The pattern instruction sheet will indicate that certain edges should be stay stitched. Following the direction of the arrows, straight stitch on single thickened fabric $\frac{1}{2}$ inch to $\frac{5}{8}$ inch from the raw edge.

Straight of grain The pattern manufacturer's key will illustrate the marking for the straight of grain. It is usually a heavy dark line with an arrow at each end. When pattern pieces are placed on fabric, this line should follow the lengthwise grain.

Tailor's tacks These are used to transfer pattern markings on to fabric. They are loose basting stitches made through two thicknesses of fabric and then cut apart.

Trim Decorative braid is sometimes referred to as trimming or trim. Alternatively, trim means to cut down. Seam turnings are usually trimmed to $\frac{1}{4}$ inch.

Underlining Lining which is used to add body to the garment fabric. It is cut from the same pattern pieces and construction markings would normally be applied to this rather than the fabric. It is then made up as one with the garment fabric.

View Each view on the front of a pattern envelope will depict a particular design. Identify the particular view you wish to make by its view number or letter.

Wrong side Look on the instruction sheet for the key where you will find an illustration of how the wrong side will be shown for making up and cutting out purposes.

Yardage box Part of the back of a pattern envelope will be boxed off and contains fabric yardage information.

Yardage requirements The amount of fabric required to make a particular design can be assessed by cross referencing the size with the view in the appropriate fabric width.

Zipper placement This is indicated on the pattern piece and is usually placed above a notch. The pattern tissue and instruction sheet instruct that the seam is left open above the notch.

Choosing the correct pattern type

When you are confronted with a pattern catalogue full of exciting and fashionable designs, it is hard to restrain yourself from immediately selecting the design you best like the look of. At this stage, however, it is essential to prevent calamity later. Each pattern catalogue contains a body measurements chart from which you should be able to determine the figure type closest to your own figure. For this, it is only necessary for you to know your height and the measurements of your bust, waist, hips and your back waist length. The chart shows where and how to take these and other body measurements for dressmaking. The chart includes a space where each measurement can be written as it is taken. As measurements tend to fluctuate from time to time, it would be advisable to write these measurements in pencil so that they can easily be rubbed out at a later date and a new measurement inserted.

Body measurement chart

	Where to measure	*Your measurement*
Height	From the floor to the top of your head. Do not wear shoes	
Bust	Over fullest part of bust, high under the arms and straight across the back	
High bust	High up across back under armpits and over the top of the bust	
Waist	At the natural waistline	
Hips	Around fullest part usually 9 inches below waist for people over 5 feet 4 inches high and 7 inches below waist for people 5 feet 4 inches high	
Back waist length	From the prominent bone at the nape of the neck to back waist	
Width across back	Over shoulder blades from armhole seam to armhole seam	
Shoulder	From neck to armhole seam at shoulder point	
Front waist length	From base of neck at shoulder over the bust to the waistline	
Shoulder to bust	Across base of neck at shoulder to the most prominent point of the bust	
Width across front	Across the chest half way between shoulder and bust line from armhole seam to armhole seam	
Sleeve length	From shoulder point over bent elbow to wrist	
Shoulder to elbow	From shoulder point to elbow	
Elbow to wrist	From elbow to wrist bone	
Upper arm	Round fullest part of upper arm	
Front skirt length	At centre front, from the natural waistline to desired hem length	
Back skirt length	At centre back from the natural waistline to the desired hem length	
Crotch depth	From natural waistline at centre front through crotch to natural waistline at centre back	
Thigh	Around the fullest part	
Inside leg	With legs apart from crotch down inner leg seam to desired finished length	
Trouser side waist length	From natural waist at side seam over hip to desired length	

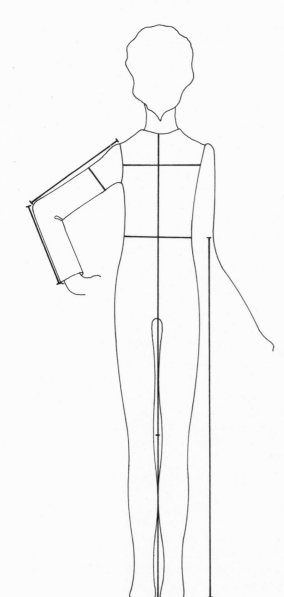

Few of us are lucky enough to conform exactly to the standard body measurements in every respect and therefore minor pattern alterations might be necessary prior to cutting out. Fitting, however, will always play an important part in your dressmaking.

Pattern manufacturers recommend that you purchase a pattern by your correct bust size taking your other measurements into account, and not by your ready to wear size or age. Bear in mind, however, that when purchasing foundation

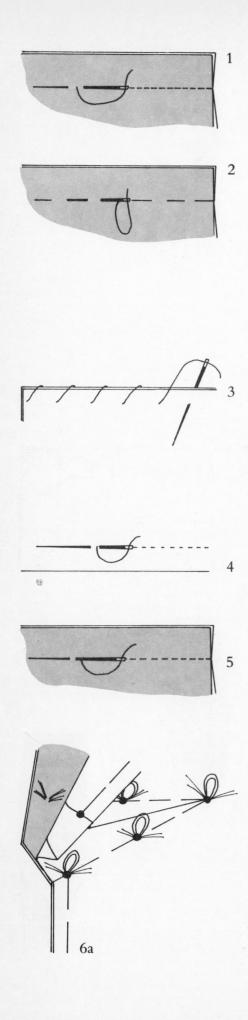

1

2

3

4

5

6a

garments, 12 women, all of whom measure 36 inches at bust level, could all take different sized brassières. You will know from the cup size of brassière you purchase, whether small, medium or large cup, how your figure relates. If you take a small cup or a large cup brassière, select a pattern by your high bust measurement and make a pattern alteration for a large or a small bust, provided measurements, such as your waist and hip are suitable for the particular pattern size. As an example, if your body measures 27 inch waist and 38 inch hips and 38 inch bust and you take a large cup size, your high bust measurement may be 36 inches. You should then select a Misses' pattern size 14 and make an adjustment for a large bust. Do not be put off by the names given to some pattern types such as Junior Petite or Miss Petite. These are not to denote age, simply a figure type. Equally, a half size pattern denotes a particular type of figure and is not, as the name might imply, halfway between two other pattern sizes. If you are in any doubt at all as to which pattern type is the correct one for you, contact the paper pattern manufacturer who will help.

Having decided which pattern type you are, you are then ready to select a design from the pattern catalogue. When you look at the catalogue and see how it is split up into sections for the different body types, you will appreciate why it was first of all necessary to determine your figure type. Some sections may be further split up into fashions for the younger person and fashions for a more mature person. From now on it is up to you to select a design which you like in your correct pattern size and type.

Basic stitches

It is advisable to know a few basic stitches prior to cutting out your fabric and starting to sew your garment together.

Back stitch is a very strong stitch which used to be used for sewing garments together by hand. It is worked from right to left by taking a needle up through the fabric and out towards you. Re-insert needle $\frac{1}{8}$ inch to the right of your thread and take a stitch $\frac{1}{4}$ inch long drawing thread through. For the next stitch the needle is inserted an $\frac{1}{8}$ inch back from this point (diagram 1).

Basting or tacking Knot thread and bring needle and thread up through fabric towards you. Take stitches of an even length, about $\frac{1}{4}$ inch to $\frac{1}{2}$ inch according to the thickness of the fabric, and ensure that the space between them is the same length as that of the stitch (diagram 2).

Overcast stitch This is the usual stitch used on raw edges to prevent them from ravelling. Work from left to right making small diagonal stitches approximately $\frac{1}{4}$ inch apart and $\frac{1}{8}$ inch to $\frac{1}{4}$ inch in depth (diagram 3).

Prick stitch or hand picking This is often used to give a garment a hand finish. It is a version of back stitch, but instead of going back an $\frac{1}{8}$ inch each time, only go back over 1 or 2 threads forming a tiny surface stitch (diagram 4).

Running stitch This is a basic stitch used for making gathers or tucks by hand. Use a milliner's needle which will take several stitches at one time and weave in and out of the fabric forming small even stitches and even spaces, before pulling the needle and thread through (diagram 5).

Tailor's tacks These are used to transfer pattern markings to fabric. In their basic form they are worked with a long double thread. A small stitch is taken through the pattern and both the fabric layers leaving a thread end approximately 1 inch long. A second stitch is taken over the first, leaving a long loop and the thread cut to leave a further 1 inch (diagram 6a). The loop is then cut through the centre, so that the pattern can be removed. Pull the two pieces of fabric apart gently and cut the threads in the middle leaving an even amount on both pieces of fabric (diagram 6b).

Continuous tailor's tacks are also made with a double thread. This is formed in exactly the same way as a basic stitch but every second stitch a loop is left of approximately 2 inches. The two layers of fabric can then be pulled apart to flatten the loops and the threads cut in the middle (diagram 7).

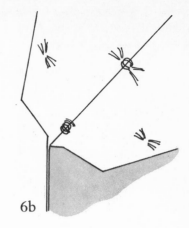

6b

Basic processes

An alternative method of transferring pattern markings to fabric to tailor's tackings is dressmaker's carbon paper. Some dressmakers find it both easier and quicker particularly if a large number of markings are involved.

Using commercial carbon paper Assuming that your fabric is cut out, right sides together, and still has the pattern pieces pinned to it, cut off two pieces of tracing paper, slightly larger than the area of the markings. Place one piece right side uppermost underneath the bottom layer of fabric and insert the other piece the right side down between the pattern tissue and the top layer of fabric. Pin the layers together firmly to prevent them from slipping. Using a tracing wheel, follow the marking lines using sufficient pressure to form a light imprint on the fabric. You can discover how much pressure is required by testing on sample scraps of fabric. Occasionally a tracing wheel will not give a sufficiently heavy marking and then the blunt edge of a knife may be used. For straight lines, guide the instrument alongside a ruler.

Pin basting It is not always necessary to go through the stages of pinning and basting before machining two pieces of fabric together. A process known as pin basting can combine the first two processes and save considerable time. The only proviso is that your machine must have a hinged presser foot. Insert pins at right angles to seam line taking up only a small amount of the fabric. The pin points should face towards the centre of the garment leaving the heads nearest to the raw edge so they can be removed quickly and easily after stitching (diagram 8).

Stitching an open seam Thread your sewing machine with an appropriate thread according to the manufacturer's instructions. Using two thicknesses of spare fabric, test stitch length and tension. Raise presser foot, place work on the bed of the machine with raw edges to the right hand side of the machine needle. Lower presser foot on to the work so that stitching lies just to the right of the basting line. Leave thread ends of approximately 2 inches to 3 inches at both ends of the seam to be neatened. To neaten thread ends by machining, start machining $\frac{1}{2}$ inch down from the beginning of the stitching line and reverse the machine back to the beginning. Set the machine to stitch forward, stitch over your reverse stitches through to the end of the seam line and again set the machine in reverse to stitch back for about $\frac{1}{2}$ inch. Thread ends may then be clipped off close to the fabric (diagram 9).

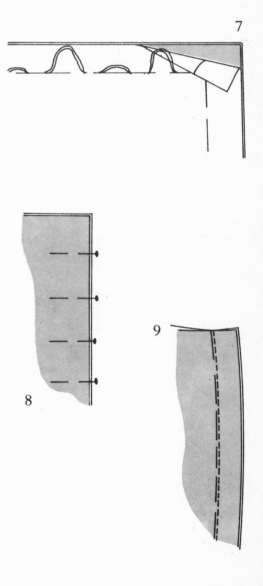

7

9

8

47

Neatening a seam After a seam is formed by machine stitching on the seam line, the seam should be pressed open and the raw edges neatened. This is very quickly accomplished by running a line of straight machine stitching $\frac{1}{4}$ inch from the raw edge along the length of the seam turning and then pinking the fabric outside this stitching with pinking shears (diagram 10).

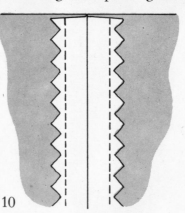

10

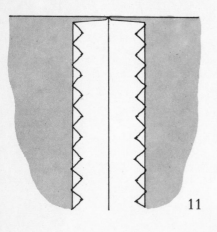

11

12

This method, however, is not suitable for all fabrics and if a hand finish is desired, the raw edges may be neated with overcast stitches. One method which is only suitable for light weight fabrics, is to turn under $\frac{1}{8}$ inch of the seam turning and straight stitch close to the folded edge (diagram 11). If you own a swing needle machine, and are using a firmly woven fabric, use the zig-zag stitch on your sewing machine to neaten the edges. Some machines also include a step stitch which is particularly useful for neatening the seams on loosely woven fabrics and knits. The machine will stitch small stitches to form a serpentine and provide a neat and firm finish.

Stitching a dart It is important to remember when stitching darts that the purpose of a dart is to give shape to your garment. They enable an otherwise flat piece of fabric to fit gently round the curves of your body. Darts should not, therefore, be stitched in a straight line but stitched from the wide end in a very gentle curve towards the point where the stitching tapers off to nothing. Clip threads and tie a knot in them close to the end of the dart (diagram 12).

16

17

18

SKIRTS AND TROUSERS

Sew a skirt

Having learnt the basic essentials of sewing, it is now time for you to cut out and sew your first successful garment. Nothing is more inspiring to the beginner than to complete a garment fairly quickly and wear it proudly.

Gather together your cutting out and marking equipment, the requisite length of fabric and your pattern. You are now ready to cut out. If your fabric has been folded up, press out creases with a steam iron and lay fabric flat on your cutting area. Remove the tissue pattern pieces and instruction sheet from your pattern envelope and following your instruction sheet carefully, set aside the pattern pieces you will require returning the others to the pattern envelope. Make any necessary fitting adjustments to the pattern, as described in the previous chapter. If the pattern tissue is excessively creased, it should be ironed flat. Read the key on the instruction sheet to make sure you understand the meaning of all the symbols. Then, taking care to observe any special notes which may be printed for the cutting layouts, find the correct cutting layout for the view you are making in the correct size and fabric width. Pencil a circle around this cutting layout immediately so that you can refer to it easily. You are now ready to pin the pattern pieces on to the fabric.

Cutting out If the cutting layout which you are following, shows the selvedges away from you with the fold nearest to you and the length of the fabric running from left to right place the fabric before you in exactly the same way (diagram 1 overleaf). The pattern pieces can now be pinned on to the fabric following the layout illustration. To ensure that each pattern piece is accurately placed on the straight of grain, measure from the fold or from the selvedges to the grain arrow and check that this measurement is the same throughout its length. If a pattern piece does not have a grain line, it will indicate that it should be placed to the fold, in which case the solid line should be placed to the fold. To keep the pattern pieces as flat as possible and thus ensure the greatest accuracy, they should be pinned in position with pins at right angles to the cutting line. If the cutting layout

65

indicates, that one pattern piece should be cut on a single thickness fabric, the pattern piece will extend beyond the fold of the fabric. In this case it is necessary to cut out the other pieces and return to pin and cut this piece later. Many dressmakers put off the moment when they must actually cut into the fabric with the shears, and not unnaturally, as this is the point of no return. However, there is no need for concern if you first of all count up all the pattern pieces which are pinned on to your fabric and include the one which is waiting to be pinned on to single thickness later. Refer to your instruction sheet to find out how many pattern pieces are required to make that particular view and you should find that the two totals are the same. As a further check, you can start working from the pattern pieces at one end of your own cutting layout towards the other end reading off all the pattern pieces which you have used and tick them off on your instruction sheet in pencil. Any mistake will come to light quickly and easily at this stage, and if no mistakes appear, you can continue to cut out with complete confidence. Use your bent handled cutting out shears and cut firmly with long strokes and not little snipping movements. Shorter strokes will be inevitable for cutting round curves and in small areas. As you cut, use your free hand to keep the fabric flat. This will prevent inaccuracy caused by the fabric lifting and stretching. Never use pinking shears for cutting out. Notches should always be cut outwards into the margin and never inwards to the seam allowance. A common short cut is not to cut them at all, but for the small amount of time it takes to cut them out correctly, this is false economy because they form an easy and quick method for matching seams correctly.

Marking The construction symbols can be quickly, easily and extremely accurately transferred on to the fabric by the use of commercial carbon paper. Select the colour which is closest to that of your fabric and test it on a scrap. Take the front of the skirt with the pattern piece still pinned to it and mark the darts

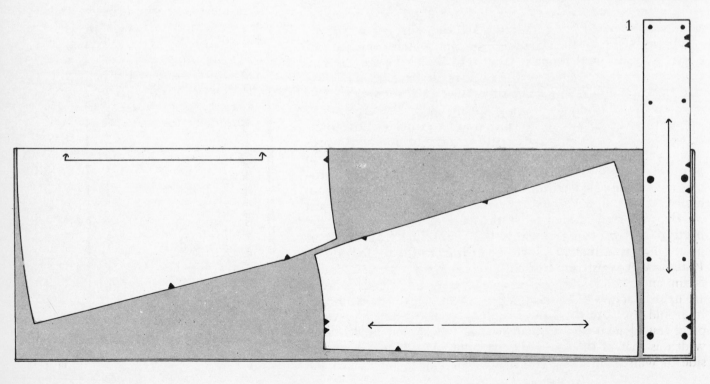

and all construction symbols (diagram 2). For a beginner it would also be advisable to mark in the waist seam. The same items should then be marked on the back. Remove the pattern piece from the skirt front, stay stitch the waistline $\frac{1}{2}$ inch from the raw edges and stitch the two darts. Now remove the pattern piece from the skirt back and again *stay stitch* the waistline $\frac{1}{2}$ inch from the edge and stitch the darts (diagram 3). The darts in the back of the garment will always be slightly longer than those in the front. As the skirt back is in two separate pieces, they should now be stitched together to form the centre back seam. Place the two pieces of fabric right sides together and pin baste, remembering that the seam will only be stitched to within 7 or 8 inches of the waistline, leaving the rest open for

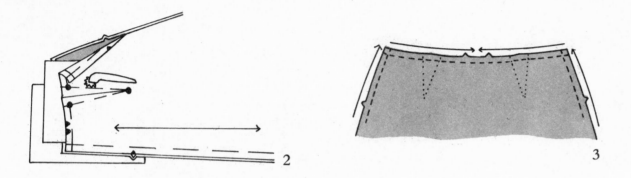

2

3

the zipper. A notch will probably mark this point. The centre back seam should now be pressed open and all darts pressed towards the centre.

Centre back lapped zipper Place the skirt back on a table right side uppermost, with the hem nearest to you and waistline away from you. Push all seam turnings towards the left hand side and fold the top left hand section of the skirt back towards you as far as the end of the line of stitching. Place the zipper face down on the right side of the skirt with the tape $\frac{1}{8}$ inch from the raw edge. The top of the zipper tapes will be level with the raw edges at the waistline and the lower tapes, which extend beyond the zipper, should be spread either side of the stitching line (diagram 4a). Baste into position. Using the special zipper foot on your machine, with the needle on its left, stitch as close to the teeth as possible starting at the bottom and working up towards the waist line. Press seam turning and zipper tape back in position on right side of skirt and press under $\frac{5}{8}$ inch seam turning on left side of skirt. Still with right side of work facing you, baste left side of skirt over left hand zipper tape so that it just overlaps the right side of the skirt (diagram 4b). Starting at the bottom and working towards the waist line, top stitch in position approximately $\frac{3}{8}$ inch – $\frac{1}{2}$ inch from the folded edge.

Waistband A waistband normally requires some form of interfacing and a heavy non-woven could be used, but better results are usually achieved by using a petersham or grosgrain ribbon. It should measure the same length as your waistband pattern piece less $1\frac{1}{4}$ inch (the seam allowance twice), and be the same width as that of the finished waistband. Attach to the wrong side of waistband along the unnotched edge $\frac{5}{8}$ inch from the

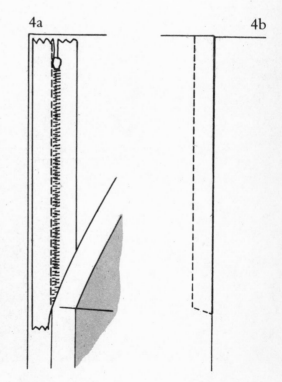

4a

4b

raw edges (diagram 5a). The other side runs down the centre of the waistband. The petersham ribbon can now be held in position by catch stitching round it, or running a line of machine stitching $\frac{1}{8}$ inch from the centre fold, or by machine basting round all four sides of the petersham. Fold the waistband right sides together along the fold line and stitch ends as indicated (diagram 5b). Clip seam at lap line, trim seam turnings to $\frac{1}{4}$ inch and trim corners. Turn waistband through to right side

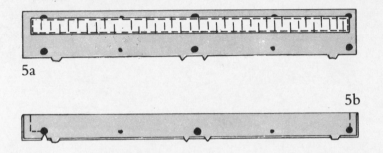

5a

5b

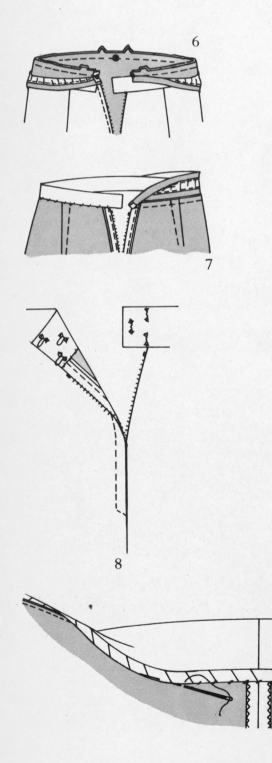

6

7

8

9

using a small pair of scissors to help you push out the corners if necessary, and press (diagram 6). With the right sides together pin waistband to skirt matching notches carefully and back edge of zipper to lap line. The skirt pattern pieces measure slightly more than the waistband itself and need to be eased on to the waistband. Baste, stitch and trim seam turnings to $\frac{1}{4}$ inch. If a particularly heavy fabric is used, these may need to be layered. press seam turnings towards band. Working from the wrong side of the garment turn under $\frac{5}{8}$ inch along raw edge of waistband and slip stitch to the seamline (diagram 7). Press the finished waistband flat and attach hooks and eyes (diagram 8). *Hem* Pin up the hem on the hem line to see that the skirt is the correct length and the hem even. If it is not, enlist someone else's help or use the type of hem gauge which you can operate yourself. Make sure that the depth from the hem line is even all round and trim off any surplus. About $\frac{1}{4}$ inch from the raw edge run a line of fairly long machine stitches around the hem. Pull thread ends to draw up stitching until the hem lies flat and press, shrinking out the extra fullness. Still working from the wrong side of the garment, stitch one edge of bias binding $\frac{1}{4}$ inch from the raw edge along one fold of the bias binding, around the hem. To complete the hem slip stitch the other folded edge of the bias binding in position (diagram 9). To slip stitch, take up one thread of the garment, and then slide the needle along for $\frac{1}{8}$ inch to $\frac{1}{4}$ inch inside the fold of the turned edge.

Pressing hems Try to avoid pressing over the hem edge. To do so first shrink out fullness, if necessary, by placing strips of brown paper between the garment and the hem and shrink out the gathers from the hem. Brown paper can be removed and hem edge neatened. Hem is then sewn in position. Final pressing is than completed by pressing from the lowest part of the garment up to the neatened hem edge, but not over it.

You now have your first garment complete and ready to wear and this will surely inspire you towards greater things particularly when you remember that from now each garment will seem quicker and easier to make.

Patch pockets as a simple addition to an A-line skirt

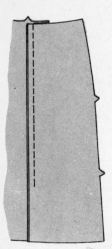

10

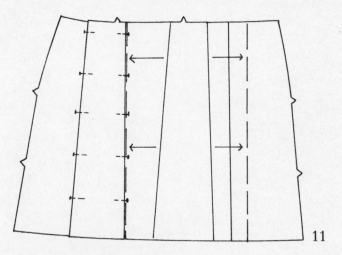

Skirt with pleats

You are already familiar with selecting the appropriate pattern pieces, following your instruction sheet, cutting out and transferring the usual pattern symbols on to your fabric. Further important construction symbols will be marked on your pattern pieces to help you form the pleats. The symbols which manufacturers use to indicate pleat and fold lines, vary considerably but here, a solid line will indicate the fold line and a broken line the one to which the fold will be brought to form the pleat. Trace these symbols on to your fabric in the same manner as before, and use a ruler to keep your lines straight. The same order of construction will apply, that is, first of all stay stitching at the waist line, and then stitching and pressing the darts. The next step is to stitch the side fronts to the front and the side backs to the back, carefully matching the notches and construction symbols (diagram 10). Press both seam

11

turnings towards the side seams. Lay garment right side uppermost on the table and form pleats by folding the fabric on the solid lines and laying the fold along the broken line, matching the construction symbols (diagram 11). Pin and baste pleats in position and then topstitch down as far as indicated, leaving the pleat release below this point basted in position (diagram 12). The pleats are now formed in exactly the same way for the back.

12

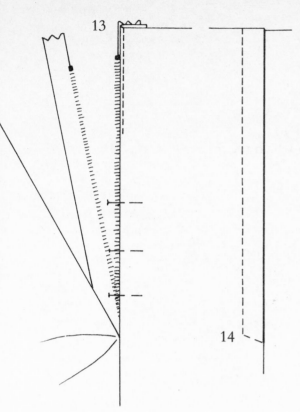

13

14

Side seams Stitch right hand side seam throughout its length matching the notches. Stitch left side seam leaving it open as indicated on the pattern piece above the notch for the zipper. *Lapped zipper in side seam* This time you can insert a lapped zipper very similar to the one on the 'A' line skirt but here, instead of stitching the right hand zipper tape to the garment from the inside, it can be top stitched through from the right side of the fabric. Press under $\frac{5}{8}$ inch seam turning on skirt back and with the zipper teeth lying just to the left of the folded edge, stitch as closely as possible to the zipper teeth (diagram 13). With the zip closed, and $\frac{5}{8}$ inch seam allowance turned under on the front, lay the front folded edge over the back seam edge so that it just covers the line of top stitching. Close the zipper teeth. Pin zipper tape firmly to fabric, baste $\frac{3}{8}$ inch from the folded edge and stitch in position (diagram 14).

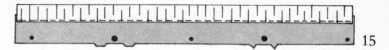

15

Waistband To achieve neat finish for the waistband which will also help to eliminate bulk when using heavier fabrics, back the fabric with a petersham or grosgrain ribbon. To do this the pattern must be adjusted slightly. Fold waistband pattern piece in half and cut out allowing $\frac{5}{8}$ inch seam turning from this folded edge. Transfer construction symbols from pattern to fabric and cut a length of petersham or grosgrain ribbon the same length as the waistband. Lap the ribbon $\frac{5}{8}$ inch over the raw edge of the fabric and stitch in position as closely as possible to the edge of the ribbon (diagram 15). With the right side of the waistband to the right side of the skirt, pin the waist seam matching the centre fronts, centre backs and all notches (diagram 16). Baste and stitch waistline seam. Trim turnings to

16

17

$\frac{1}{4}$ inch and press towards waistline. Turn back the raw edges on the front and back of the waist band $\frac{5}{8}$ inch or so that they are level with the zip opening (diagram 17). Fold over petersham

71

and pin. Now pin and slip stitch the petersham over the waist-line seam on the inside.

Hem On this particular pleated skirt the hem can be taken up in part in the normal way but where seams interrupt the pleats a special hem technique is used. Particular care should be taken to ensure that the raw edge of the hem is neatened in such a way that it will provide as flat a finish as possible so that it will not show through to the right side after the pleats are pressed. The step stitch on a swing needle machine is excellent for this purpose. Alternatively the raw edge may be stitched ¼ inch from the raw edge and then pinked.

Hem for pleats with seam interruption By forming hem in the usual manner and pressing seam turnings open, even if the seam turnings are layered, it is not usually possible to press the pleats and form a sufficiently sharp pleat. An easier method is to stitch such seams to within approximately 8 inches of the lower cutting edge so that the garment may be formed and fitted at this level and the waistband attached. The hem level must then be adjusted and the hem allowance turned up. The seam can then be stitched through to the lower edge of the hem and the threads securely fastened (diagram 18). To neaten the seam turnings and ensure that they will not show below the hem, it is advisable to use the zig-zag stitch on your machine and coming up from the stitching line at the lower edge of the hem at an angle to the raw edges of the seam turning where the seam may be neatened in the usual manner (diagram 19). Trim away the lower corner of seam turning.

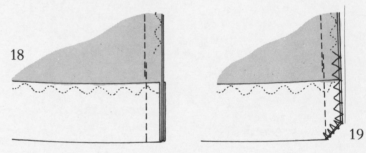

18

19

Fold back remainder of hem about ⅛ inch to ¼ inch and blind stitch to skirt. Take up one thread from the garment and a small stitch from the hem at even intervals and make sure that you do not pull the thread too tight.

Trousers with a waistline facing

Trousers have formed one of the most important fashion trends for some years now and have become an accepted part of a woman's wardrobe rather than an item of clothing in which it was excusable to do the gardening or take a walk on a wintery day. Trousers are elegant, can be made in a wide variety of fabrics and are designed to suit most shapes and sizes. Patterns for trousers are excellent and you need have no fear of poor results, but you should bear in mind when selecting a pattern that the designs which are simpler to sew, such as those with an elasticated waist, will not provide you with the same close-to-the-body fit unless the pattern is designed to be sewn with 'knit' fabrics only. If you like to wear your trousers closely fitting, it is advisable to select a pattern which does not have a conventional waistband because trousers with a waistline facing, or those which are finished with shaped petersham ribbon, tend to be more comfortable when you sit down. The pattern should be selected to your correct waist and hip measurements and any adaptations should be made to the pattern tissue before cutting out.

Follow the cutting layout carefully and cut out all the pattern pieces before transferring the pattern markings to the fabric. Stay stitch as indicated on the instruction sheet, stitch darts and press towards centre (diagram 20). At this point a tailor would set the creases by first of all steam pressing them in position and then pounding with the pounding block. However, unless you know that no fitting adjustments will be necessary, it is not advisable for you to do this yet as the creases may be thrown off centre by any fitting adjustments.

The next stage would normally be to stitch the inner leg and side seams and thereafter insert the zipper. However, as an invisible zipper is to be inserted into the side seam here, it will be easier to complete this process first and stitch the seams thereafter.

Inserting an invisible zipper Exchange your regular presser foot for the special grooved foot which is used for inserting invisible zips.

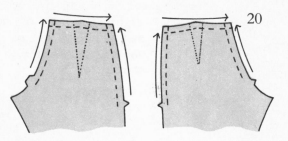

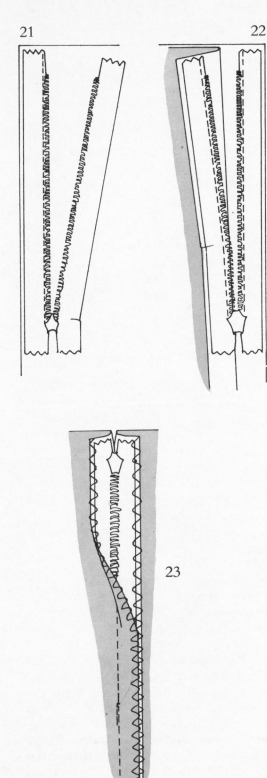

Keep the waistline of the trousers and the top of the zipper away from you and lay the open zipper face down on the right side of the trousers back with the zipper teeth running along the seam line (diagram 21). The outer edge of the zipper tape should face towards the outer edge of the seam allowance. The top of the zipper should be set $\frac{1}{4}$ inch below the waist seam line. Stitch this side of the zip in position by running the right hand groove of the zipper foot over the zipper teeth. The foot will automatically set the needle such that your stitching line is correctly positioned. Stitch down as far as the zipper pull tab, remove work from under machine and finish thread ends. Place the other side of the zipper face down on the trousers front with the zipper teeth running along the seam line (diagram 22). Check to make sure that the top of the zipper is set $\frac{1}{4}$ inch below the waistline seam and then stitch, this time using the left hand groove of the zipper foot as far as the zipper pull tab. Remove work from machine and fasten thread ends. Replace special zipper foot on the machine with the regular zipper foot, close zipper and place fabrics right sides together. Start to stitch side seam where zipper stitching ends and stitch on the seam line for at least 2 inches. The zipper presser foot may then be exchanged for the regular presser foot and the remainder of the side seam stitched. The lower edges of the zipper tapes should now be fastened to the seam allowances with machine or hand stitches (diagram 23).

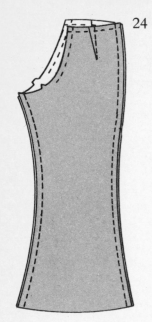

24

With fabric right sides together and matching notches carefully the inside leg seams may now be stitched and the side seam of the right hand leg (diagram 24). Neaten the raw edges and press the seams open.

The simplest method of stitching the crutch seam is to place one leg inside the other with the right sides together and use a very small machine stitch (diagram 25). This seam may be reinforced with a second row of machine stitches half an inch from the raw edges between the notches. Trim the seam allowance between the notches to $\frac{1}{4}$ inch and clip; press remaining seam turnings open.

Waistline facing Because the trousers have a side fastening, the facings will both have been cut placed to a fold. Transfer construction symbols to fabric and remove pattern pieces. Stay stitch waist seam line and place front facing right side uppermost with the waistline curve away from you on the table (diagram 26). Lay back waist facing over it, wrong side uppermost (right sides together) again with waistline curve away from you. As you look at this work, it is the side seam to your right which should be stitched together. After seam is stitched, the lower

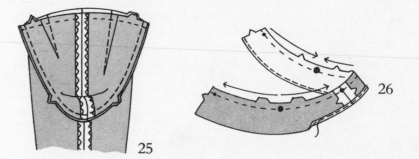

25

26

unnotched edge of the facing should be neatened and then the facing is ready to apply to the garment.

With the right sides together, pin and stitch the facing to the garment matching notches and side seam (diagram 27). To eliminate bulk at the waistline it is a good idea to layer seam turnings. Clip to stitching line and press seam turnings towards the facing. Working from the right side of the garment, understitch the facing to the seam allowances close to the seam line.

27

This will help to form a sharp edge at the seam line and prevent facings from showing when the garment is worn. Turn facing back to the wrong side of the garment and pin in position. Turn back $\frac{5}{8}$ inch seam allowance on the left side of waist facing and hold in position with hemming stitches to zipper tapes (diagram 28). The waist can now be fastened at the uppermost point of the waistline facing with a hook and eye.

Hem It only remains to adjust the trousers for length and finish the hem. The raw edge can be neatened with a zig-zag stitch

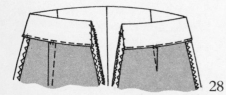

28

and the trouser hems sewn into position with a lock stitch. A trouser hem can easily be caught when you are putting your foot in and out of a trouser leg and this stitch is particularly strong to prevent this from happening. Work from left to right and secure a knotted thread in the hem. Run thread along hem for $\frac{1}{4}$ inch and take up one thread from the garment and a small stitch from the top of the hem pulling the needle through over the looped thread (diagram 29). Stitches should be formed at approximately $\frac{1}{4}$ inch intervals.

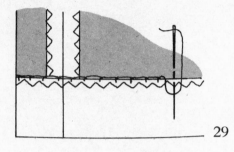

29

Pressing in the creases Crease lines will sometimes be marked on your pattern tissue in which case you simply need to transfer these lines to your fabric and to press the creases firmly in position remembering to use your clapper board. If no crease lines are marked, place trousers side on to the ironing board and make sure that all side and inner leg seams run along the ironing board on top of one another. Smooth the fabric out from this point and lightly press folds for your trouser creases. Try the pants on to ensure that these creases are in the correct position and if so return them to the ironing board and press firmly. It is well worth while taking the time to press the creases in firmly at this stage so that afterwards they will always hold in position firmly.

Trousers with an elastic waist casing

A number of trouser patterns are designed with an elastic waist casing. These will not provide the same smooth close fit at waist and hip level unless the pattern is designed for 'knits' only when the fit is usually excellent. This is, however, an excellent way to enable you to sew trousers extremely quickly and easily. They are best worn with a tunic or long sweater worn outside the waist and over the hips.

To introduce you to 'knit' fabrics the trousers illustrated are made up in a 'knit' but exactly the same order of construction will apply to woven fabrics. Some sewing machines incorporate a special stretch stitch especially for sewing 'knit' fabrics. If your machine does not have one, a narrow zig-zag stitch should be used for all seams and remember to use the correct thread. This provides the seam with stretch so that when the fabric stretches, the seam may also. If seams on a 'knit' fabric are stitched in the usual manner for woven fabric, the stitching is likely to break when it comes under pressure. It is also wise to remember that seam turnings will probably not require neatening.

Stitch the centre front and centre back seams using the narrow zig-zag stitch and if extra reinforcement is required, stitch again this time $\frac{1}{2}$ inch from the raw edges. Trim seam

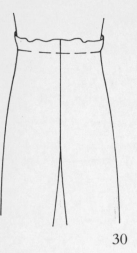

30

turnings between notches and press the remainder of the seam open. Pin baste side seams and inner leg seams and stitch.

Fitting Already the trousers are ready for you to try on and fit. The place where the trousers are most likely to need adjustment, is in the crotch depth, but instead of making this adjustment at the crotch the trousers are adjusted at the waistline. The trousers should be lifted until they feel comfortable at the crotch, but make sure they are not so tight that you will be unable to sit down. Tie a tape round your natural waistline and mark this point on to the trousers. After you have removed the trousers, mark above this point the waistline casing allowance (usually 1 inch to 1½ inches) and trim away the excess (diagram 30). If the trousers are too large elsewhere, increase the amount in the seam turnings but make sure that an even amount is taken out from both sides. If the trousers have been raised to change the crotch depth, it is likely that the trouser hems will also need adjustment. Pin trousers to the desired finished length.

The waist casing A new fold line will have been formed if you adjusted your trousers for the crotch length. Press the casing allowance to the inside of the garment and stitch ¼ inch from the raw edge leaving a 2 inch opening at the centre back through which the elastic can be inserted. Cut a piece of elastic of a length to fit comfortably round your waist, plus 2 inches. And with a safety pin fastened to one end, thread the elastic through the casing finally pinning both ends together with the safety pin (diagram 31). The trousers can now be tried on again to check for comfort at waist level. The elastic can then be stitched in position by hand or machine (diagram 32). Stitch up the opening in the casing enclosing a tape in the stitching to mark the centre back of the trousers (diagram 33).

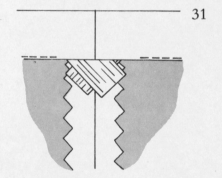

31

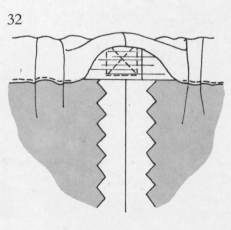

32

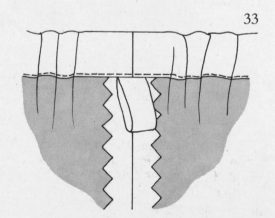

33

Match shirt to trousers for casual elegance

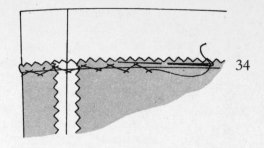

34

Hem All garments made up in a 'knit' fabric should be allowed to hang for 24 hours before the hem is sewn up. Trousers can be pegged on to the lower bar of a wire coat hanger. After 24 hours, try on to see if the hem has dropped and adjust if necessary. Stitch the raw hem with a straight machine stitch $\frac{1}{4}$ inch from the edge. A catch stitched hem is usually best for knitted fabrics because it will move in the same manner as the fabric (diagram 34). Fold the hem back to the line of straight stitching on the hem. Working on the wrong side and from left to right, make a small stitch from the hem pulling the needle in on the right and taking it out on the left. Keeping the thread away from you take the next short stitch in the garment approximately $\frac{1}{4}$ inch away. Continue in this way until the hem is completed, straighten hem and press.

An alternative type of waistline facing which you may encounter does not exclude the use of a zip. This method of construction is excellent for woven fabrics as it provides them with much better shaping than the previous method but is equally good for knit fabrics as well. The zipper is usually inserted in the centre back with the top of the zipper $\frac{1}{4}$ inch–$\frac{3}{8}$ inch below the lower line of stitching on the waistline casing.

Inserting the zip The centre back seam is stitched as far as the construction symbol for the zipper. Lightly press under the $\frac{5}{8}$ inch seam turnings. Working from the right sides of the fabric

35

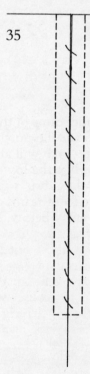

and with the zipper right side towards you, pin the closed zipper under the folded edges such that they both meet at the centre of the zip teeth. Baste firmly in position and then to prevent the folded edges from pulling apart during machining, oversew them together with large hand stitches (diagram 35). Attach the special zipper foot to the machine and starting on the right hand side of the zip, with the machine needle to the left of the zipper foot, stitch right round the zipper using the basting as a guide.

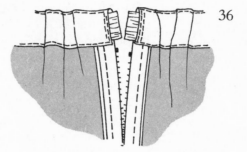

36

The elastic casing will be formed in a similar way with a casing allowance folded over to the inside of the garment. Form two lines of machine stitching as indicated, usually approximately $\frac{1}{8}$ inch from the top folded edge and $\frac{1}{8}$ inch from the lower raw edge. Cut the elastic to the desired waist measurement, plus 2 inches, and insert with the aid of a safety pin through the opening in the centre back of the casing. Adjust to fit and hold in position with a line of machine stitching continuing upwards from the zipper stitching (diagram 36). Sew hooks and eyes on the inside of the waist casing for the waistline fastening.

Crease line for knit trousers Crease lines do not always form as easily in knit fabrics as they do with woven fabrics. If this is the case, the creases can be stitched into position after the crease lines have been determined stitching as close to the edge of the crease as possible. This will also help to prevent the knees from bagging.

Trousers on a yoke

This trouser design is ideal for evening wear and the fact that it has a yoke incorporated as part of the design means that waist darts are no longer necessary.

The side seams of the trousers front and back should be stay stitched from the notch upwards and along the upper cutting edges. The yoke will also require stay stitching at the waistline edge as well as the lower edge.

With the fabric right sides together stitch the centre back and centre front seams of the trouser. Press open above notches and trim away below. Now attach the front yoke to the front trouser with the right sides of the fabric together and making quite sure that the notches are correctly matched (diagram 37). A common mistake here is to try to attach the waistline seam to this seamline but this will not occur provided the notches are matched. The trouser will need to be eased onto the yoke then basted before stitching. This process is repeated for the back. You are now ready to stitch the side and inner leg seams and insert the zipper.

To complete the yoke, the processes are exactly the same as

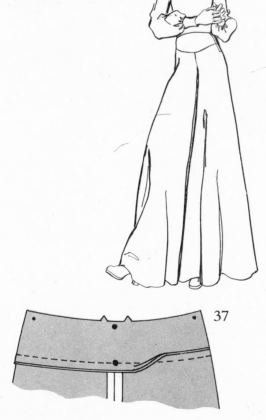

37

for applying a waistline facing. The pieces of fabric are stitched together at the right hand side seam but the lower edges of the facing need not be neatened. Attach the facing at the waistline (diagram 38). Trim turnings to $\frac{1}{4}$ inch, clip and press towards facing. This part of the yoke may now be turned to the inside of the garment. Lightly press back the $\frac{5}{8}$ inch seam turning all round and pin to the zipper tapes and around the stitching line at the lower edge of the yoke. Hem in position and form waistline fastening with a hook and eye (diagram 39).

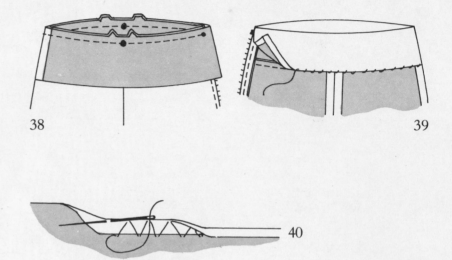

Rolled hem Because the trousers are widely flared, it is likely that you will have selected a lightweight fabric for a soft effect in which case a rolled hem should be formed. Decide on the finished length for the trouser and trim away the hem allowance except for $\frac{1}{2}$ inch. Stay stitch $\frac{1}{8}$ inch to $\frac{1}{4}$ inch from the edge and trim close to the stitching. Roll the hem twice between your fingers to form a narrow roll of no more than $\frac{1}{4}$ inch and slipstitch (diagram 40).

42

49

DRESSES

A sleeveless dress

It may well be that having examined your figure in front of a mirror you find that you are lacking in height or maybe your waist is somewhat larger than you would wish. You might therefore decide to keep the amount of separates in your wardrobe to a minimum and build up a co-ordinating and versatile wardrobe around dresses instead. Not unnaturally you would prefer to start learning to sew making a simple one-piece dress and nothing could be simpler or more versatile than a shift dress without collar or sleeves. Once you have learned to sew this particular dress you will soon find out that exactly the same processes apply in making a pinafore or tunic dress, a most useful addition to any wardrobe, allowing you to ring the changes frequently with different sweaters and blouses. From there it is a very short stage to sewing a dress which includes a horizontal seam. This need not be at the waistline and a very good point to break up the line of the dress is just below bust level forming an empire line design

The design illustrated is quick and easy to sew but need not be dull and boring. The simplest designs are often the most chic but if you prefer something more interesting, it is easy to trim the dress either with your own accessories or with braid.

Select a firm fabric of medium weight which does not stretch and does not lack body. At the same time purchase all your thread and haberdashery requirements and when you get home prepare your sewing area for action.

Cutting out You will probably only have four pattern pieces to cut out; front, back, front facing and back facing. Pattern manufacturers often incorporate the neck and armhole facing into one so that the garment is quicker to sew. The front facing is usually cut out with the centre front placed to a fold and the centre back of the back facing is left with a seam allowance because the centre back opening will neaten the zip at the upper edge. Refer to the cutting instructions in the previous chapter. If you are dubious as to whether your layout is correct, double

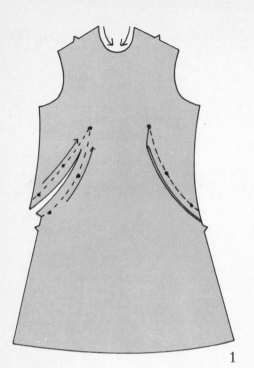

1

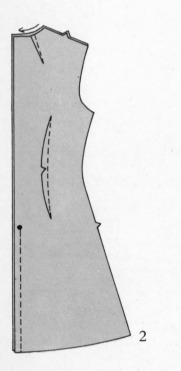

2

check to make sure that you are using the correct pattern pieces. As it is not possible for a paper pattern to show different cutting layouts for every single size of each view, they will often show one illustration for the largest size stating that smaller sizes should be cut to the same layout but with pattern pieces interlocked more closely. Now you can check to see whether your pattern pieces are interlocked as closely as they might be, still making sure they are placed on grain. Thirdly check the width of your fabric. Is it the width you thought it was? Maybe it was sold to you as 54 inch width fabric and it only measures 52 inches. This is a point which few people ever think to check and with good reason too because usually if there is any doubt about the width of the fabric, the manufacturer will always quote the narrowest possible width. The next stage is to query the yardage quoted on the back of the pattern envelope with the manufacturer in question. It is exceedingly unlikely that an incorrect yardage will slip through the many checking processes through which a pattern must pass prior to going out on sale. However, it is always worth checking with them because you may just have found one of those very rare errors.

Cutting out should normally present no problems provided you adhere to the basic rules and follow the instruction sheet. *Marking* The construction symbols on the pattern could be transferred to the fabric with the use of tailor's tacks but here again it is probably easier to use dressmaker's carbon paper. The amount of construction symbols on such a design will be limited but make sure that all small, medium and large dots are clearly marked. Once the garment is unpinned from the tissue pattern pieces, you are left with no guide lines whatever to help you match the seams accurately. With tracing paper, marking only takes a very short time and is well worth the effort. Remove pattern pieces from the fabric.

Making up the dress It is not strictly necessary to stay stitch the neck and shoulders of a dress such as this but if it makes you feel safer shoulder seams should be stay stitched starting at the neck line stitching out towards the armhole and the neckline should be stitched starting from the shoulder towards the centre. The darts, however, should be stay stitched. Start from the side seam and stitch towards the point of the dart. Remove fabric from under the machine. Stitch the other side of the dart in exactly the same direction. The back waist darts in the back of the dress need not be stay stitched.

Darts Pin front darts making sure that the dots are very accurately matched and easing the fabric where necessary. Stitch carefully into position and press towards centre (diagram 1). Pin and stitch back shoulder darts and long back waist darts then pin and stitch the centre back seam as far as the zipper opening and press open (diagram 2). Press the darts towards the centre making a small clip at waist level in the back waist darts. Press back $\frac{5}{8}$ inch seam allowance along zipper opening and neaten the raw edges of the back seam with the zig-zag stitch to prevent them from ravelling.

Centre zip insertion Working from the right side of the garment place the closed zipper with the right side towards you behind the zipper opening with the seam turnings pressed back and and top of the zipper set $\frac{1}{4}$ inch below the neck seam line

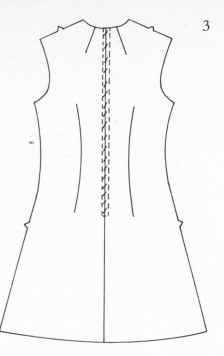

(diagram 3). Pin into position. The two folds of fabric should meet at the centre of the zipper teeth. From this point you can continue to insert the zipper by hand. Starting from the bottom end of the left hand side of the zipper, prick stitch $\frac{1}{4}$ inch from the centre fold up to the neckline removing pins as you go. On the right hand side of the zipper again start at the lower edge and work in the same manner. This method will in fact take very little longer than machine stitching the zipper in but of course it will not be as strong. If your machine stitching is good and straight, and you wish to machine stitch the zipper, you must first of all firmly baste the zipper in position. Then starting at the neck edge, use large overcasting stitches to hold the two folds of fabric together at the centre of the zip. This will prevent the two edges from pulling apart during machining. You are now ready to machine stitch the zipper into position using your line of basting as a guide. Start at the neck edge and stitch down one side of the zipper. At the lower end of the zipper, make a line of stitching at 90° across the bottom of the zipper before turning the machine through 90° again to stitch back up the other side. Make sure that your stitching is an even distance from the centre otherwise the garment will look unbalanced. Remove basting and overcasting stitches and press.

Facings If the facings for this dress were not cut in one, it would be normal to proceed and stitch the side and shoulder seams. However, as the neck and armhole facings are cut in one they are first of all attached to the garment and the side and shoulder seams stitched afterwards. The normal rule for applying interfacing is that if you use an iron-on interfacing it should be applied to the facing but any other interfacing would be applied to the garment. In this particular instance, a non-woven iron-on interfacing would be suitable. Using the facing pattern pieces cut out the interfacing, remembering that a non-woven interfacing has no grain and the grain line does not matter (diagram 4). Remove pattern tissue and iron the interfacing

4

on to the facings. Neaten the raw edges at the lower part of the facings. Identify the shoulder seam on front and back facings and press the $\frac{5}{8}$ inch seam turning towards the wrong side (the side with the interfacing). Now apply the front facing to the front of your garment making sure that the notches match and remembering at the shoulder that your seam lines should match, pin baste firmly (diagram 5). Stitch along neck and

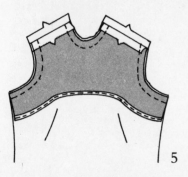

5

armhole seam lines, trim seams to $\frac{1}{4}$ inch and clip the curves. As the right side of the garment faces you with the facing over-laid on to it, run your hand between the two layers of fabric to the shoulder and pull both thicknesses through so that the fabric lies wrong side to wrong side and faced. Repeat for the other shoulder and then press the work carefully making sure that you do not roll the edges. It may help to baste the neck and armhole edges first, press lightly, and then remove the basting stitches before pressing firmly into position making sure that you press out any traces of the basting stitches. The facings for the back are applied in exactly the same manner. At the centre back the facing will extend $\frac{5}{8}$ inch beyond the centre back opening edges of the zip. Fold the seam turnings under and slip stitch to the zipper tape on the inside of the garment. At this point, whilst you are hand sewing, it is advisable to attach the hook and eye to finish the neck edge of the garment.

Shoulder seams The shoulder seams are ready to be stitched now and you will note that by pressing under the $\frac{5}{8}$ inch seam turning on the facing prior to stitching the neck and armholes, you have neatly tucked away extra fabric which would otherwise have been in your way when stitching the shoulder seams. With right sides together match shoulder seams. When stitching, it is most important that you stitch accurately along the seam line but be careful not to catch in the facing (diagram 6). You may find it easier to carry out this process using the zipper foot on your machine. Trim the seams to $\frac{1}{4}$ inch, press them open and then slip the seam turnings underneath the facings. You are then left with the two folded edges of the facings facing one another which should be slip stitched together (diagram 7). This whole process is very quickly and easily

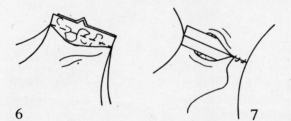

6   7

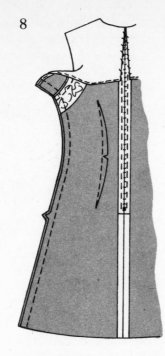

8

accomplished provided that you work accurately. It is most important that you stitch your seam turnings accurately at $\frac{5}{8}$ inch.

Side seams You are now ready to stitch the side seams with the armhole facings in one. With the right sides of the fabric together, pin the front to the back at the side seams being careful to match the notches and make absolutely sure that the seams for the armhole facings match (diagram 8). Pin basting can help enormously here because by taking up a small amount through the exact point which must match accurately, the two pieces of fabric can be held firmly in position facilitating easy stitching. Starting from the hem edge stitch up towards the armhole, over the armhole seam to the edge of the facing. Raw edges should be neatened by turning under $\frac{1}{4}$ inch and edge stitching (diagram 9). Turn the facing back towards the inside of the garment and press with the seam turnings open. At this point it is advisable to catch the facing down on to the seam turnings so that it will stay in position. Press remainder of side seams open.

Hem Different types of hem finishes have already been discussed in the previous chapter and as you continue to make more of your own clothes, you will probably develop a personal preference for particular hem finishes according to the type and weight of fabric you are using. To finish the hem, turn under $\frac{1}{4}$ inch, edge stitch then slip stitch it into position (diagram 10).

9

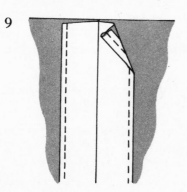

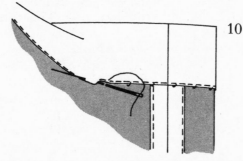

10

Equally the tailor's hem always provides an excellent finish but you are more likely to be able to catch your foot in and so bring it down. This latter method is good however if the garment is to be lined.

Dress with raglan sleeves in a 'knit' fabric

A great many basic sewing techniques have now been accomplished but the subject of sleeves has not yet been tackled at all. To start you off, a dress with raglan sleeves is usually easier than one with set in sleeves.

The pattern has been specially selected so that it is sized for 'knit' fabrics only. Select your usual pattern size by your correct body measurements and do not think that you will get away with using a woven fabric because you won't and the garment will come up much too small. The pattern includes six pattern pieces; one back, one front, one back facing and one front facing and the sleeve back and the sleeve front. This sleeve is cut in two pieces with a seam running from the neck over the shoulder and down the centre of the sleeve. Raglan sleeves are not always cut in two pieces such as this one and may sometimes incorporate a dart which runs from the neckline along the shoulder and extends approximately 1–2 inches over the point of the shoulder. The purpose is the same – to remove unwanted fullness and create the shoulder shaping. Before cutting out, check the basic rules for sewing with 'knit' fabrics and determine which thread and machine needle you will use.

Following the correct layout in the manufacturer's instruction sheet, lay pattern pieces on to fabric and cut out. It is particularly important to retain scraps of fabric for trial stitching etc. Carefully transfer construction symbols from the pattern tissue to the fabric and remove tissue pattern pieces.

Stay stitching The stay stitching on this particular garment is very important from the point of view of the design and particularly bearing in mind that you are using a 'knit' fabric. Stay stitch as indicated by the instruction sheet (diagram 11).

Constructing the dress Stitch all darts and the centre front seam as far as the opening for the neck (diagram 11). Press.

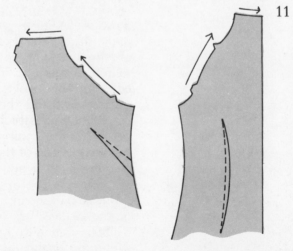

11

Now you are ready to attach the front of the sleeves to the front of the dress (diagram 12). With the right sides together, pin the two pieces of fabric together making absolutely sure that the notches match and that the construction symbols

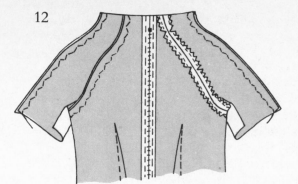

12

have been accurately matched also. Stitch from the underarm point towards the neckline accurately along the seam line. This particular seam will take a lot of stress as you move and should therefore be reinforced by making a further row of machine stitching directly over the first. Clip curves and press seam turnings open. The same processes can now be carried out on the back. Stitch the centre back seam as far as zipper opening and press open, at the same time pressing back the $\frac{5}{8}$ inch seam turning along the zipper opening. A centred zipper should be inserted in the same manner as for the sleeveless dress but because the dress has a slightly raised neckline, it will be necessary to place the tab at the top of the zipper $\frac{3}{8}-\frac{1}{2}$ inch below the neckline seamline. With the zipper inserted the back sleeves can be applied in exactly the same manner as the front sleeves.

Join front and back together at the shoulder seam and stitch. To avoid unnecessary bulk at the front of the neck, the front pattern piece has been designed with a built-in neck facing. The front facing is joined to this and faces the front sleeve and the back facing joins to this at the shoulder to face the back sleeve and back (diagram 13). With the right sides together pin

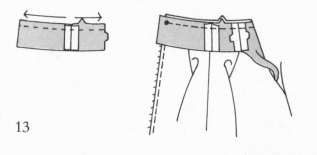

13

and stitch the front facing to the back facing and press the seam open. Working from the right side of the garment bring the front neckline extension outside the garment and with right sides together pin and stitch to the other end of the front facing. Press seam turnings open. Still with the right sides of the fabric together you can stitch the neck facing to the garment along the neck seamline making quite sure that the notches match and that shoulder seams and front armhole seams match accurately. Trim seam turnings and clip the curved edge and the corners. Press the neck seam turnings between the centre back and the shoulder towards the facing. From the right side understitch close to the seamline through the facing and the seam turnings. Neaten thread ends. Turn the facing to the wrong side of the garment and using the point of a pair of scissors to push out the corner at the centre front neck edge. The facing will extend by $\frac{5}{8}$ inch at the centre back edges. This should be turned under, slip stitched down on to the zipper tapes on the inside of the garment.

From the wrong side, press neck area carefully to avoid stretching. Hand stitch facings to the seam turnings to hold in position.

Side seams Starting from the hem edge stitch along the seamline up through the underarm point to the lower edge of the sleeve (diagram 14). Because the dress is made in a 'knit' fabric, it will

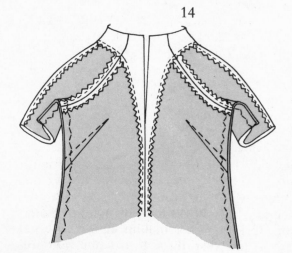

14

15

16

be necessary to clip this seam where it curves prior to pressing open.

Hems Raw edges on 'knit' fabrics do not ravel so it is rarely necessary to neaten the raw edges. To take up a hem, however, it is usually advisable to run a line of straight machine stitches $\frac{1}{4}$ inch from the hem edge and then pink the raw edge. Use a tailor's hem or catch stitch into position (diagram 15). Use the same hem finish for the sleeves. Sew two hooks and eyes, one at the neck edge and one just below it.

Shirt dress or blouse

If you have worked your way through each garment so far, you will already be feeling fairly proficient. In sewing a shirt dress you will learn about collars, setting in sleeves, making sleeve openings, gathers and cuffs, and how to make button holes. There is indeed a lot left to learn but once you have mastered the making of a shirt dress, you will have opened the doorway to making shirts, blouses, and full length evening dresses.

The fabric you choose for this garment could vary from a lightweight wool for a day dress or silk for a full length evening version or a very lightweight cotton or man-made fibre for a soft feminine blouse. As this is your first attempt at setting in a sleeve, an excellent fabric selection would be a light weight wool because this will enable you to shrink out the fullness at the sleeve head easily.

Select the appropriate pattern pieces and cut out. When transferring the construction symbols, you will encounter several new markings, in particular the slash line on the sleeve for the sleeve opening and the button holes. For a dress with several buttons and buttonholes in a line, it is usual to mark the horizontal lines for the buttonholes on to the fabric so that they are of even length and accurately in line. Bound button-holes are marked by two vertical lines one for the inner edge and one for the outer edge of the buttonhole. Remember that these markings should only be transferred on to the right hand bodice front and on the left hand bodice front it is particularly important to mark the centre front line crossed by the horizon-tal button placement lines. The point at which these two lines cross is where your buttons are sewn into position. Whenever possible, most patterns show the facing cut in one with the front, in which case a fold line will also be indicated and this should be transferred on to both sides of the front.

Following the pattern instruction sheet, stay stitch where necessary. Cut a strip of interfacing the width of the front band less seam turnings and the same length (diagram 16). A further strip of interfacing should be cut of equivalent length approxi-mately 2 inches to $2\frac{1}{2}$ inches wide.

Neaten the raw edges of the facing section on both fronts, stitch darts and press down. Working from the wrong side of the fabric, attach the piece of interfacing 2 inches to $2\frac{1}{4}$ inches wide to the facing extension of the left front. The interfacing should be ironed into position with one edge running alongside the fold line and the other extending into the facing. Interface the right front band between the stitching lines and with fabric wrong side uppermost, press under the $\frac{5}{8}$ inch seam turn-ing on the right hand side of fabric. Attach front band to right front, placing the fabric right sides together and stitch right hand seam. Press the front band over raw edges so that the folded edge runs along the fold line. Top stitch $\frac{1}{4}$ inch from each edge of the band throughout its length. Fold both front facing extensions along the fold line to the wrong side forming the facing.

Pockets Neaten the top raw edge by turning under $\frac{1}{4}$ inch and stitching. Fold upper section back along fold line with right sides together and stitch, trim turnings to $\frac{1}{4}$ inch and turn fabric through to neaten the upper section. Press remaining $\frac{5}{8}$ inch seam turnings to the wrong side, clip curves and press. On the right side of the dress front, pin pockets in position along pocket lines and slip stitch side and lower edges (diagram 17).

Collar Join the dress back and front at the shoulder seams.

Two pieces of fabric have been cut out for the collar; one is the upper collar and the other the under collar. Apply interfacing to the wrong side of the upper collar and hold in position by running a line of machine stitching $\frac{1}{2}$ inch from the raw edges. Trim the interfacing close to stitching. At the points of the collar, trim the interfacing diagonally across the points approximately $\frac{1}{4}$ inch inside the points at which the seam lines meet. Attach upper collar to under collar and stitch along the long outer edge furthest from the neck (diagram 18). Press the seam turnings towards the under collar and then understitch from the outside close to the seamline through under collar and seam turnings. Trim seam turnings and again place collar right sides together and stitch sides (diagram 19). Trim seams to $\frac{1}{4}$ inch and clip the corners diagonally before turning the collar right side outwards. Use the points of a pair of closed scissors to help you push out the points of the collar. These should always look sharp and even and here a poor finish could let your garment down.

Two pieces of fabric have also been cut for the collar band; outer collar band and inner collar band. Interface the outer collar band and stitch $\frac{1}{2}$ inch from raw edges. Trim interfacing close to stitching and place right sides together to underside of collar (diagram 20). Be quite sure that construction symbols are accurately matched here so that the neck will fit well. On the inner collar band press under the $\frac{5}{8}$ inch seam turning at the lower edge, trim seam turning to $\frac{1}{4}$ inch and clip curve. This band is now attached to the upper collar and the seam line stitched through all four thicknesses (diagram 21). Trim seam turnings and clip curves before turning the fabric right side out. Press firmly.

Attach whole collar unit to dress fabrics right sides together pinning the collar band to neck edge. Stitch, trim and pay particular attention to trimming the corners at the front of the dress so that you have a neat finish at this very obvious point. Press seam turnings towards the band and then bringing over the inner collar band with the lower seam turning pressed under, slip stitch the edge over the seam line (diagram 22). Stitch side seams. Hang the dress on a hanger to avoid unnecessary creasing whilst you complete the sleeve unit.

Sleeves A sleeve opening is marked at the lower edge of the sleeves and the traditional method of neatening these is to form a continuous strip opening. Many patterns, however, have now devised methods to avoid this process as some sewers find it complicated. No difficulty should be encountered provided

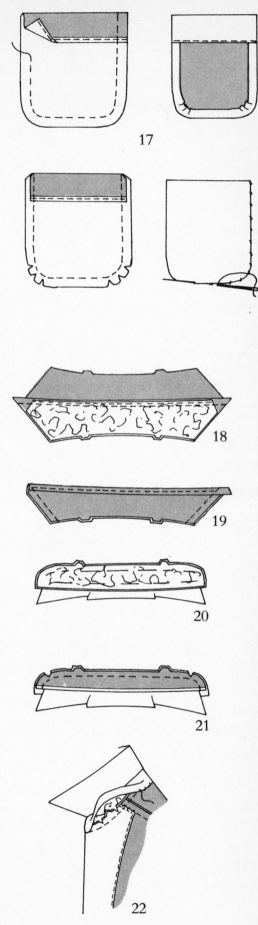

17

18

19

20

21

22

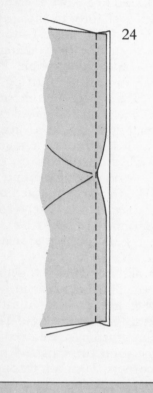

23

24

you stitch accurately. An alternative neatening process is, however, described later in the chapter, should you prefer to look this up.

Stay stitch along the slanted lines using a small machine stitch and taking one stitch across the point (diagram 23). Slash between lines of the stitching right up to stitching line at point. Spread the V shape such that it forms a straight line and if you find that it does not, this will mean that you did not clip closely enough into the point. Cut a strip of fabric long enough to face this edge and $1\frac{1}{2}$ inches wide. On one side of the strip press under $\frac{1}{4}$ inch and attach the other side of the strip to the slashed edge with the right side of strip to the right side of sleeve. The strip will have a $\frac{1}{4}$ inch seam turning throughout but the stitching line for the slashed opening should follow the stay stitching line. The point is therefore placed $\frac{1}{4}$ inch from the raw edge of the strip. Stitch slowly taking great care when you reach the point and then press seam turnings away from sleeve towards the strip (diagram 24). Now bring the folded edge of

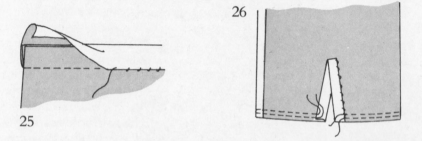

26

25

strip over on top of the seam line and slip stitch by hand (diagram 25). The continuous strip opening is now complete and will not be visible from the right side of the garment when it is being worn. The openings will be pressed in a different way for each sleeve but remember that the front edge is tucked under and place over the back edge.

Two rows of ease stitching are run around the sleeve head between the notches, the first row on the seam line and the second row $\frac{1}{8}$ inch to $\frac{1}{4}$ inch from this. Leave the thread ends loose as these are used to pull up the stitches later. Stitch and press underarm seams. At lower edge, starting at the opening run one row of gathers along the seamline to the other side of the opening, with another row $\frac{1}{8}$ inch to $\frac{1}{4}$ inch from this (diagram 26).

Cuff It is always advisable when working cuffs, to do both cuffs at one time rather than completing one and then going back to the other. Always remember that your cuffs are like opposites because they will be attached one to a left sleeve and one to a right sleeve so they should be formed as opposites.

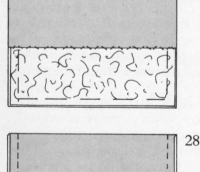

27

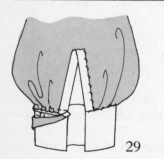

28

29

Attach interfacing as indicated (diagram 27). On inner cuff edge, press under the $\frac{5}{8}$ inch seam turning and trim to $\frac{1}{4}$ inch. With right sides together, stitch sides as indicated, trim and turn through (diagram 28).

Pull up the gathering threads slightly and then with the fabric right sides together, pin to the cuff matching the construction symbols. Adjust gathers until lower edge of the sleeve fits cuff exactly and then secure the ends of the gathering threads around a pin. Stitch seam, press turnings towards cuff. Slip stitch the folded edge of inner cuff over seam line (diagram 29).

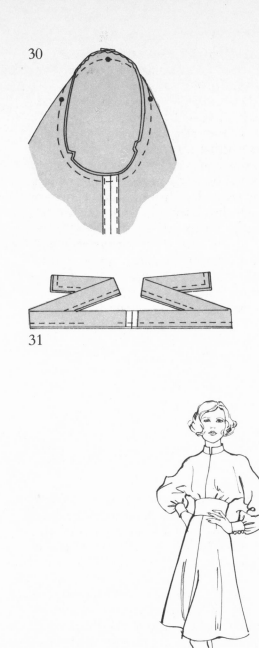

30

31

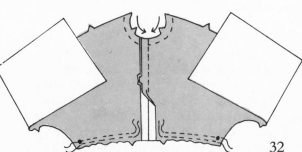

32

Set in sleeve Hold dress inside out and the sleeve right side out. Drop the sleeve through the armhole of the dress and the fabrics will now be right sides together ready for you to work from the inside and attach the sleeve to the armhole. The first step is to pin the two pieces of fabric together in six places: 1. underarm sleeve seam to side seam of dress; 2. double notches together at the back; 3. single notches together at front; 4. dress shoulder seam to construction symbol at the top of sleeve head; 5. match front and back construction symbols. From here on it is a simple process to pin the underarm curve of the armhole because the two pieces of fabric should fit exactly together. Above this point draw up ease stitching slightly to bring the size of the sleeve head down to the side of the armhole. Gathers should not be formed. This is simply a method of reducing a little fullness and easing the sleeve head into the armhole. Pin carefully as indicated, baste and stitch in position starting at the underarm seam and working round the sleeve remembering that once you reach the notches, your line of stitching will run over your inner line of ease stitches (diagram 30). To reinforce the underarm of the sleeve, make a further line of machine stitching from the single notch through the underarm to the double notch. Trim seam turnings close to the second line of stitching. Remaining seam turnings need not be trimmed but should be pressed from the wrong side over a tailor's ham. Only the seam turnings are pressed together and not the sleeve, to shrink out extra fullness from the sleeve seam turnings to match the armhole turnings.

Tie belt The two pieces of fabric should be seamed together across the width and pressed (diagram 31). Fold belt in half lengthwise with the right sides together and stitch as indicated leaving an opening at the centre to turn the belt through. This is an instance where only a $\frac{3}{8}$ inch seam turning is allowed to obviate excessive trimming. Trim the seam turnings and pay particular attention to trimming the corners. Turn belt through the opening, press under the $\frac{3}{8}$ inch seam turnings along both edges of the opening and slip stitch together. Press carefully.

Hem Try the dress on to check the hem length and remember to tie the belt so that you have an accurate indication of the finished hem length. Check also the button and buttonhole placements. Take up the hem, and fold back front facing on to the hem and slip stitch down.

Buttons and buttonholes Hand worked or machine buttonholes would be suitable, but for this dress, with so many, it would be quicker to use a machine. Lap fronts right over left. Cuffs lap front over back. Make buttonholes in the upper part, and sew buttons to lower part. For accurate instructions for a machine buttonhole refer to the sewing machine instruction booklet.

Dress featuring a stand up collar, Dolman sleeves and a midriff band

A design such as this is suitable only for soft fabrics which drape well. The crisp effect of the stand up collar is repeated with a midriff band nipping in the waist. Soft shaping is evident throughout the bodice and sleeve area and light gathers are used to produce the soft bust shaping (diagram 32). The skirt repeats this softness with a gently flaring 'A' shape but will probably require underlining.

Bodice The only new process here is that the sleeve seams are

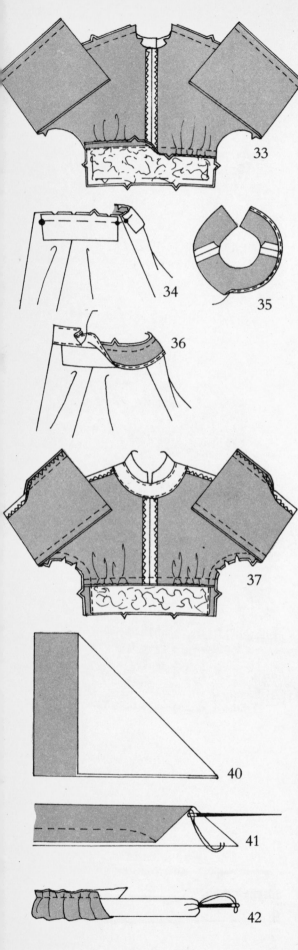

stitched in one with the side and shoulder seams (diagram 33).

Collar Four pieces of fabric have been cut out for the collar. Two of these should be interfaced on the wrong side and the other collar pieces applied to them right sides together. The edges are stitched. Trim seam turnings and corners and clip curves. Then turn the collar sections through right sides outwards, press and baste the raw edges together along seam lines. Baste in position on neck edge then form the neck facing (diagram 34), remembering to neaten the unnotched edge (diagram 35). Apply the facing in the usual way but over the collar, stitch and press back (diagram 36). The collar will now automatically stand up in position (diagram 37).

Patch opening An alternative sleeve opening is to cut a patch of fabric 1 inch longer than the opening and usually $2\frac{1}{2}$ inches wide. Two of the long edges and one of the short edges should be neatened and the patch laid over the marking for the opening, right sides together. From the wrong side stitch the 'V' shape as before then slash the opening to the point (diagram 38). Turn through to the wrong side and then press before catching the outer edges of the patch lightly down on to the fabric (diagram 39).

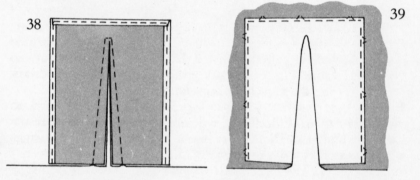

Rouleau loops A decorative method of forming the cuff fastening is with rouleau loops and ball buttons. Loops can be made from purchased cord or self fabric. To make self fabric loops, cut strips of fabric on the true bias $1\frac{1}{8}$ inches wide (diagram 40). Fold in half lengthwise with the right sides together and stitch $\frac{1}{4}$ inch from the fold stretching the fabric slightly whilst you stitch (diagram 41). If you are using particularly heavy fabric, it will be necessary to stitch a greater distance from the fold. At one end of bias strip, slant stitching away towards raw edges and secure. Using a strong needle and thread, make two or three stitches in the fabric at this end of the bias strip and use the blunt end needle to pull the fabric through the tunnel and thus turn it right side out (diagram 42).

Measure the size of loop required by looping over the button and cut to this measurement plus $1\frac{1}{4}$ inches. On the right side of the fabric place the loop in position with both ends level with the raw edge of side front of cuff (diagram 43). Stitch and turn cuff so that loops are caught into the seam.

Cuff The gathers are formed in exactly the same manner as for the shirt dress and the cuff attached.

Skirt The skirt on the dress is a simple 'A' line. Form the skirt in the usual manner, and with right sides together pin skirt to the midriff band, stitch and press turnings towards band (diagram 44).

Zipper closing The zipper can be inserted according to the method you favour, but a hand finished zipper would provide a suitable finished effect. Insert a lapped zipper and instead of machine stitching the left side, prick stitch the zipper by hand (diagram 45). Finish back of stand up collar with hooks and eyes (diagram 46).

Midriff lining The dress will fit closely to the midriff and therefore should be lined to make it more comfortable to wear. The lining is cut from the same pattern pieces and seamed at the sides. Press under the $\frac{5}{8}$ inch seam allowance on upper and lower edges and $\frac{3}{4}$ inch along centre back edges. Trim all turnings to $\frac{1}{4}$ inch and then with the dress inside out pin the midriff band lining in, wrong sides together. Slip stitch folded edges to stitching lines.

Hem Complete the hem and your dress is ready to wear.

Underlining

A dress is underlined or mounted on to a lining to give it added body or strength. A loosely woven fabric unless made up into a full flowing gown, will require an underlining to keep the garment in good shape. It will prevent a skirt back from seating out whereas the otherwise loosely woven fabric would probably stretch and seat. Underlining is also used to provide extra body and weight to a fabric. For instance if a brushed rayon were selected for a tailored dress, it may be necessary to mount the fabric on to an underlining to provide the necessary weight to give shape to the garment.

Lining of any sort seems to indicate a lot of extra work to the sewer but an underlining will not create much because the garment and underlining are sewn as one. No construction symbols need to be transferred on to the fabric itself but only on to the underlining. Each underlining piece of fabric is placed with its wrong side to the wrong side of the corresponding garment piece. The garment is then made up in exactly the same manner (diagram 47). Stay stitch round each piece of fabric $\frac{1}{2}$ inch from the raw edges to hold the underlining firmly to the top fabric. Alternatively run lines of loose tacking in a vertical direction approximately 4 inches apart on each piece of fabric. This method may be necessary on very fine fabrics because stay stitching might cause the seam edges to draw up. Test on sample scraps of fabric before starting on the garment.

An excellent way to neaten raw edges of seam turnings on a garment to be loose lined is to use bias strips of lining fabric.

Binding seams Cut strips of bias lining and join as indicated until they measure the length of the seam (diagram 48). The seam should be pressed open first and one edge of the bias strip should be placed right sides together with the garment fabric on the seam turning. Stitch $\frac{1}{4}$ inch from the raw edges, trim turnings slightly and press seam towards bias strip. Press under $\frac{1}{4}$ inch along remaining raw edge of bias strip and place folded edge over previous seam line. Edge stitch close to the fold to hold in position (diagram 49).

Sleeves It is not normally necessary to underline the sleeves unless a particularly loosely woven fabric has been selected. If, however, this does prove necessary, remember that there will be four fabric layers rather than two to incorporate into the arm-

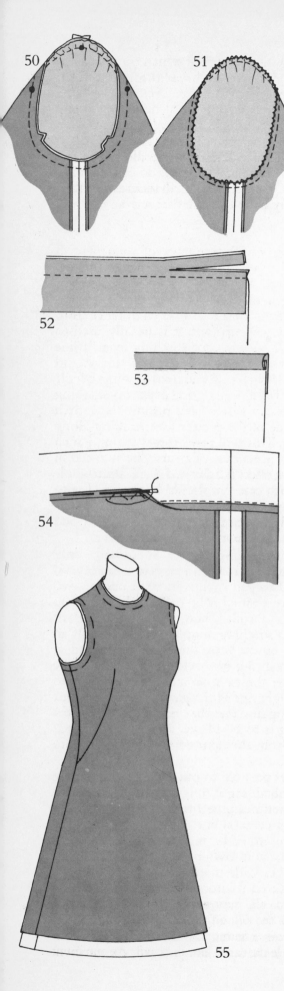

hole seam (diagram 50). The seam turnings will require trimming and neatening either by means of a seam binding or a machined zig-zag stitch (diagram 51).

Hem The neatest hem finish of all is a bias bound hem and the method for forming this is very similar to that which you use when binding seams. Join bias strips to the measurement of the entire hem. With the right side of the bias strip facing the right side of the fabric on your turned up hem, stitch the two together $\frac{1}{4}$ inch from the raw edges (diagram 52). Trim and fold the strip over the raw edges to the wrong side of the hem (diagram 53). Working from the right side of the fabric, stitch as closely as possible to the turned edge of the bias strip (diagram 54). Provided you stitch sufficiently closely to the turned edge of the bias, the stitching will hardly show. Press firmly and then blind stitch the hem into position making stitches in the lining and in the machine stitching on the underside of the hem. Hem stitches cannot possibly show through on the right side of the fabric and provided the hem is pressed carefully, the finished effect on the right side of the fabric should be perfect. This method of binding a hem is eminently suitable for any garment.

Loose linings

To make a dress really comfortable to wear and give it a wonderfully professional and neat appearance inside, a loose lining can be used either in addition to an underlining or simply to line an outer fabric only. The lining is constructed quite separately from the garment itself and usually in the same manner and is attached to the dress at points such as the armhole, neckline and zip opening. The basic shell of the garment should be made up in both outer fabrics as well as lining fabric to the same stage, that is, with no sleeves, collars or facings attached. It is not normally necessary to neaten the raw edges of the seam turnings in a loose lining because the seams are inside the garment and get very little wear. This is one of the times when a dressmaker's dummy or dress form will be of most help to you. After the zip is inserted into the centre back of the garment, the dress should be placed on the dressmaker's dummy inside-out with the zip fastened (diagram 55). Place the lining over this with the right side outermost and pin the two pieces of fabric together around the neck and each armhole taking care that the shoulder seams and the underarm seams are accurately matched. At the centre-back where the zipper has been inserted, the lining will have been left open. Turn back $\frac{3}{4}$ inch seam turnings at centre back and pin the folded edge onto the zipper tapes (diagram 56). Afterwards a collar or facings can be attached to the garment in the normal manner. If the garment has a sleeve, the sleeve should be set-in in the normal manner and the lining hand-stitched to the seam line thereafter. This process is clearly described in the next chapter for lining a jacket or coat.

Hems should be taken-up separately but held loosely together at each seam by swing tacks or chain tacks.

Swing tack A quick method of forming these is to secure a thread in the hem of the garment at a seam point and take several small stitches using a double thread (diagram 57). Take a small stitch leaving a loop of two or three inches (diagram 58a). Holding the needle in your right hand, use your left hand to pass through

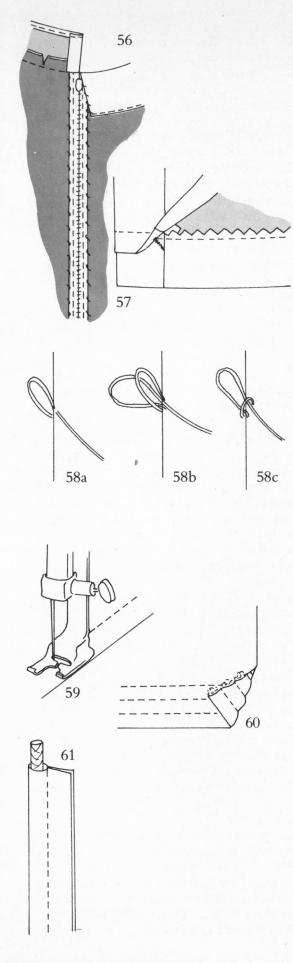

56

57

58a   58b   58c

59   60

61

the loop, pick up the thread (diagram 58b) which runs between the fabric and the needle and draw this thread through to form another loop tightening the first (diagram 58c). In the same manner reach through the second loop with the left hand and draw out a third. Continue until the chain is approximately an inch to an inch and a quarter long then draw the needle through the last loop and tighten to secure. Using the needle and thread in the usual manner attach this end to the inside of the lining hem at the equivalent seam. Take several small stitches and then secure the thread end firmly to make sure that it does not pull away during wear.

Top-stitching

Top-stitching can be used to attach one piece of a garment to the other if the part which is to be overlaid has first of all been faced. The fabric is then placed such that the upper part overlaps the lower part and the garment is stitched together by means of stitching through from the right side at an even distance from the faced edge. For decorative purposes, it is usually used to emphasize seaming detail. To keep your stitching even, a line of basting stitches can first of all be inserted and this should then be followed closely. However, if you own a swing-needle machine, the easiest method of making good even top-stitching is to set the machine needle in the left hand position and stitch the work with the right side of the presser foot running along the seam line (diagram 59). This will form top-stitching $\frac{3}{8}$ inch from the seam line. The process can, of course, be worked in reverse. A better decorative effect is achieved if silk buttonhole twist thread is used, in which case this should be threaded onto the bobbin as well as the top of the machine. Making good top-stitching requires very little practice if formed in this way and can add a very expensive touch to the dresses you make.

A particularly expensive finish which is usually only incorporated into model or couture garments is to form several layers of top-stitching and to pad them out with one or two layers of lambswool to give a raised rolled effect (diagram 60). This finish can be used for a collar, belt, the lower edges of sleeves and hems. The top stitching should always be half an inch apart at least because by the time the fabric has rolled, it will give the appearance of being narrower. Simply insert the layers of lambswool inside the hem or collar and base into position. Stitch from the right side of the garment three or four rows of top stitching making sure that the lines of stitching meet accurately. If this stitching is to be placed around a hem, it is usually advisable to start from the hem edge working up into the garment.

Piping seams It is sometimes possible to purchase corded piping but if you have difficulty obtaining it, it is very simple to make your own. Seams are sometimes piped to accentuate seaming detail and particularly on a princess line dress, this can be very slimming. The piping can either be in a toning colour or a complete contrast. To make your own piping, you will require bias strips of fabric $1\frac{1}{4}$ inches wide made up into a continuous length and cord. Encase the cord into the centre of the wrong side of the bias strip, match the raw edges, and baste the two pieces of fabric together to the side of the cord (diagram 61).

To insert the piping into a seam, lay the folded part containing the cord just outside the seam line towards the garment

111

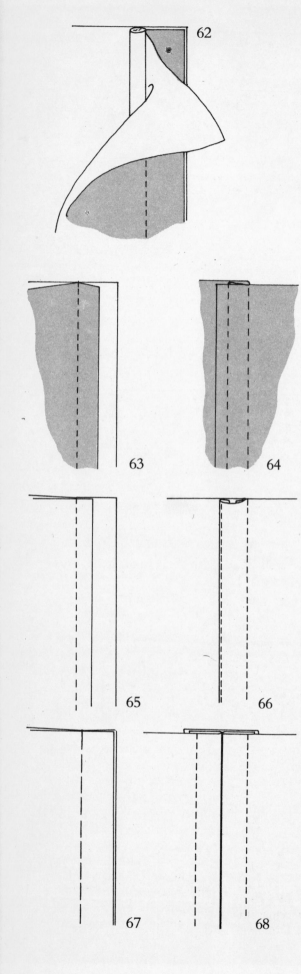

62

63

64

65

66

67

68

with the raw edges facing the same way as the raw edge on the garment. Baste into position along seam line and make the seam in the usual way with the fabrics right side together (diagram 62). Some machines have a special foot for cording but if your machine does not have one, use the zipper foot to enable you to work close to the cord. Press the seams open with the seam turnings for the piping pointing to the side of the garment over a thick towel to prevent the cord from flattening and thus spoiling its decorative effect.

Welt seam This can be used to provide a decorative finish to the side of a pair of trousers. The side seam is stitched in the usual manner taking $\frac{5}{8}$ inch seam turnings which are pressed to one side and the under seam allowance trimmed to $\frac{1}{4}$ inch (diagram 63). Working from the right side, top-stitch $\frac{1}{4}$–$\frac{3}{8}$ inch from the seam line through to the remaining $\frac{5}{8}$ inch seam turning (diagram 64).

Flat felled seam A seam is made taking the usual $\frac{5}{8}$ inch seam turnings but with the wrong sides together. Both seam turnings are then pressed in one direction and the under seam allowance trimmed to $\frac{1}{8}$ inch (diagram 65). The raw edge of the upper seam allowance is then turned under by $\frac{1}{8}$–$\frac{1}{4}$ inch, laid over the trimmed edge, and top-stitched close to the fold (diagram 66). Working from the right side, make a line of machine stitching close to the folded edge. This type of seam is frequently used on reversible fabrics and provides a very strong finish for garments which will take exceptionally heavy wear.

Slot seam This is a purely decorative seam often used at the side seam for trousers or on the bodice of a dress. The seam is stitched taking $\frac{5}{8}$ inch seam turnings with machine basting press seam open (diagram 67). A strip of fabric is then placed behind the seam turnings which will later show through on the right side of the garment. It can, therefore, be a contrasting, self-fabric or toning colour. The strip of fabric should be $1\frac{1}{4}$ inches wide and equal in length to the seam. Centering the strip, place its right side uppermost behind the seam turnings and top-stitch a $\frac{1}{4}$ inch either side of the seam line through all three thicknesses (diagram 68). The seam which was originally machine basted may now be unpicked leaving the folded edges loose. This is also known as a channel seam.

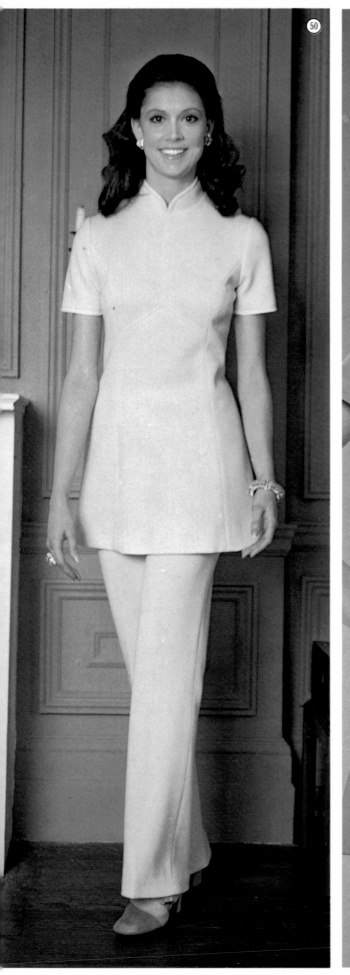

56

TAILORING

Sew a jacket

This is where you enter the realms of tailoring and learn how to mould a garment into the correct shape by the use of tailoring canvas and pad stitches. If you have never done any tailoring before, you would be well advised to go to a reputable large store and seek the advice of a trained assistant when selecting your fabric, lining, interfacing and other sewing notions. It is particularly important to seek good advice on this subject and by attending a tailoring class for beginners or an advanced dressmaking class, you could glean valuable information from your instructress.

The fabric for the garment must be medium weight at least and sufficiently closely woven to prevent the interfacing from showing through to the right side. In addition to this you should bear in mind that the garment will entail a lot of work and, therefore, the fabric should be worthy of it and provide a superb finished effect when the garment is completed and wear well for several years. You would also be well advised to bear in mind these points when selecting a pattern. A classic design will always look well. The design selected for this purpose is a jacket with princess seaming which will make fitting easier, if it is necessary, and has a single button fastening at the front. For a tailored garment it will be necessary for you to make a bound buttonhole but at least there is only one of them. Other features of the jacket include flap pockets, a notched collar, two-piece set-in sleeves and a back vent. The only real way to learn how a process is completed is to get on with the job so begin by cutting out the fabric first, then the lining and finally the interfacing. Your pattern may not include a pattern piece for interfacing the back of the jacket in which case you should make one yourself. The shoulder area on a jacket takes considerable strain and therefore requires interfacing to just below the armhole. Match the seam lines of the side back to the back of the pattern tissue. Place a piece of plain tissue over this and trace the following lines: armhole curve, shoulder seam, neck edge finishing at the centre back seam line. Draw down the centre back seam line for approximately

129

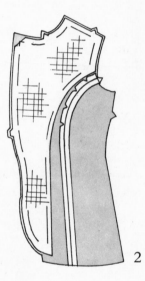

10–12 inches and curve a line as indicated from this point dropping to two to three inches below armhole (diagram 1). Draw in line from this point to the under arm. Transfer all construction symbols on to the new tissue pattern piece and remember to mark the centre back point with the symbol indicating that it should be placed to the fold. The seam down the centre back of the jacket provides ways of shaping and the back vent but as this is not required for the interfacing, the centre back seam is eliminated, reducing extra bulk.

Jacket front All stayed stitching should be carried out as instructed by your instruction sheet. To transfer construction symbols on to the fabric use tailor's tacks. Because your front is in two pieces at present, join the side front to the front and press the seam open clipping the curve so that the seam turnings lie flat. Attach the interfacing to the front remembering to clip it diagonally across the point of the revere. Machine baste in position half an inch from the outer edges and trim the interfacing close to the stitching (diagram 2).

2

The interfacing has only one free edge which should now be caught down on to the fabric using long running stitches but again only picking-up a thread from the garment fabric so that the stitches do not show on the right side.

Bound buttonhole There are several methods of forming bound buttonholes and the method you choose is more or less a matter of personal preference. The method from which it is most easy for a beginner to achieve a good finish is the 'window method' which completely neatens the raw edges leaving an oblong hole into which strips of fabric are later placed.

Window method Mark the buttonhole lines in the usual manner and then cut a piece of light-weight fabric of the same colour as the garment and measuring approximately $1\frac{1}{2}$ inches larger all round than the buttonhole markings (diagram 3a). Place the fabrics right sides together and using a small machine stitch make an oblong by stitching $\frac{1}{8}$ inch either side of the centre buttonhole marking and straight across the ends (diagram 3b). Make sure the buttonholes are of even width by

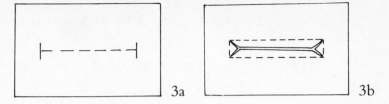

3a

3b

taking the same number of stitches at each end. Cut the button-hole open as indicated cutting right into the corners without cutting the stitching forming triangles at each end and then turn the piece of light-weight fabric through to the wrong side of the garment encasing the raw edges between the light-weight fabric and the garment fabric forming a window which will be oblong in shape. Press carefully making sure that you form a knife edge around the oblong and so that the light-weight fabric cannot be seen from the right side. The next stage is to cut two pieces of garment fabric measuring $1\frac{1}{2}$ inches by the length of the buttonhole plus an inch. These can be cut on the straight of grain but generally speaking a more satisfactory effect is achieved if they are cut on the bias. Place the two pieces of fabric together, right sides to the middle and machine baste down the centre lengthwise (diagram 3c). Press open as though you have formed a seam placing the wrong sides of the fabric together and then place this behind the oblong so that the machine basted seam shows through the window along its centre (diagram 3d). Pin through from the right side of the

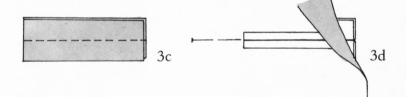

3c

3d

fabric to the patch to hold firmly in position. Do not baste. The garment fabric only is then folded back leaving the light-weight fabric, the encased raw edges and the patch. Stitch through these thicknesses over the previous line of stitching as indicated on both long sides of the buttonhole and then, folding the fabric back along the short side, stitch across the triangle, and through the light-weight fabric and patch (diagram 3e). The buttonhole is now held firmly in position and needs no further attention at this stage. However, after the facing has been attached, you will need to carefully locate the position of the buttonhole, and slash the facing fabric along its length through the centre (diagram 3f). Make a small clip at the centre of each slash and then turn back the edges and hem securely in position forming an oval shape (diagram 3g). Remove machine basting from buttonhole.

3e

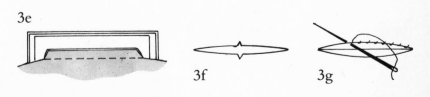

3f

3g

Patch method This is the traditional method of forming bound buttonholes. Cut a patch of the garment fabric on the bias measuring two inches by the length of the buttonhole plus 1 inch. The patch is then attached to the right side of the fabric over the buttonhole marking and carefully pinned in position, right sides together. Working from the wrong side of the garment, stitch the outline of the buttonhole forming a rectangle and making sure that you stitch the same number of stitches down each side (diagram 4a). Cut the buttonhole through the centre and then out to each corner forming the small triangle at each end but making sure that you cut as far into each corner as possible without cutting the stitching. The patch of fabric can now be pulled through to the wrong side of the garment and the narrow seam turnings formed by cutting the buttonhole open should be pressed away from the opening. To form the edges for the buttonhole, work again from the right side of the fabric and form a small fold from the patch so that it extends half way across the buttonhole. Hold in position by prick-stitching along the seam line through the two thicknesses of fabric making sure that the stitches are not pulled too tight, otherwise small indentations will show on the right side. Form a fold of fabric from the other side of the buttonhole in exactly the same manner and again prick stitch, then over cast the rolled edges together along the centre of the buttonhole. From the wrong side of the buttonhole it remains to oversew the triangular ends of the buttonhole on the patch (diagram 4b).

4a

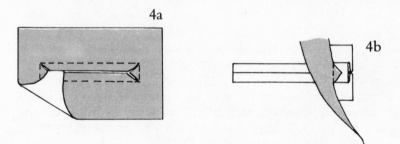

4b

Press lightly with the over casting stitches still in position then remove these carefully before pressing again to remove any impressions made in the fabric by the over-casting stitches. The buttonhole is neatened in exactly the same way as before when the facing is attached.

Piped buttonholes This method of making buttonholes requires a certain amount of practice but very little finishing is required and, therefore, many home sewers find it quick and reliable.

5a   5b

Measure the finished width of the buttonhole and for each buttonhole cut two strips of fabric twice the finished width of the buttonhole by its length plus 1 inch. These may be cut on either the straight or the bias grain. The strips are folded in half and accurately basted down the centre (diagram 5a). Press them carefully and lay them on the right side of the fabric either side of the centre of the buttonhole opening with the raw edges towards the centre and the folded edges away from it. It is important that these strips be accurately positioned so that your line of basting stitches falls immediately over the outer markings for the buttonhole. Stitch in position as indicated forming a double row of machine stitching and then turn the work over so that you cut the opening from the wrong side (diagram 5b). Cut down the centre of the buttonhole and out to the corners forming the triangle as before (diagram 5c). Then the piping strips can be turned through and the folded edges at the centre of the buttonhole held together with over-casting stitches until the garment is completed. Still working from the wrong side of the garment, fold back the garment fabric and stitch the triangle left by the diagonal cutting to the piping strips to reinforce the ends of the buttonhole (diagram 5d). The buttonhole will again be neatened in exactly the same manner when the facing is attached.

5c   5d

Welt pockets with flaps Many garments are illustrated with flap pockets but some of these do not in fact form a proper pocket and are purely for decoration. It is only when a welt pocket is formed in addition to the flap that the pocket is useable. The construction symbols on your pattern tissue will appear like a giant bound buttonhole and all construction symbols on the flap, the pocket and the garment itself are of prime importance so that you achieve a neat finish. The first stage is to form the flap by interfacing the wrong side of one piece of fabric and then, placing both flaps together, right sides to the middle, stitch along seam line around the three sides as indicated. Trim the seam allowance and corners and clip the curves before turning the flap through so that the right sides are outside and then press. Top stitch $\frac{1}{2}$ inch from the finished edges and then baste the flap along the pocket line making sure that the construction symbols are accurately matched. Trim the raw edges of the flap to a $\frac{1}{4}$ inch. Now fold the welt strip in half lengthwise with the wrong sides together and baste along the lower pocket line such that the raw edges face the raw edges of the flap extending over the pocket line by $\frac{1}{4}$ inch (diagram 6a). Make sure that the welt is well centred so that it extends beyond the pocket line an even amount both sides (diagram 6b). Your pocket will have been cut out in lining fabric and this should now be placed over the flap and the welt with the right side of the pocket to the right side of the garment. Stitch through all thicknesses along the length of the pocket lines but do not stitch across the ends. Both the pocket and the jacket should now be slashed in exactly the same manner as for a bound buttonhole, clipping diagonally out to the corners leaving a triangle. It is

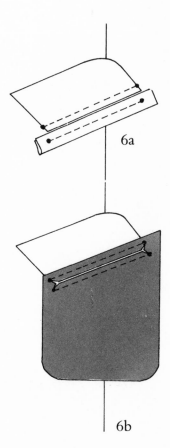

6a

6b

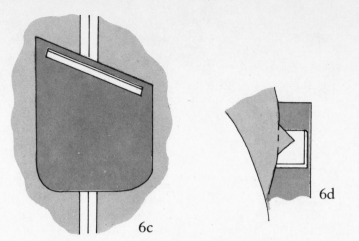

6c

6d

easier to slash the pocket separately from the garment and it is most important that you do not cut either the welt or the corners of the flap. Turn the pocket through to the wrong side of the garment through the slash bringing with it the raw edges of the flap and the raw edges of the welt (diagram 6c). These will lie between the wrong side of the pocket and the wrong side of the garment. Press carefully and from the inside fold back the side of the pocket and stitch the small triangle to the welt on the inside (diagram 6d). Now that the sides of the pocket opening are secured the remaining pocket section can be placed right sides together with the pocket and stitched on all sides (diagram 6e). From the right side of the garment the pocket flap can now be pressed down and then so that the flap will remain in this position, top-stitch through all thicknesses an $\frac{1}{8}$ inch above the seam of the flap (diagram 6f).

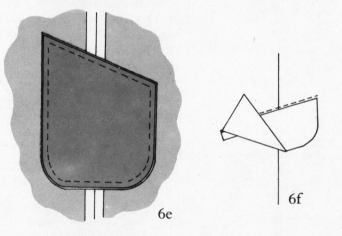

6e

6f

Jacket back It seems strange after so much work to go back to stay-stitching and forming darts. It is none the less necessary and afterwards the centre back seam can be formed. The jacket has a vent at the centre back and the instruction sheet instructs you to reinforce the corner where the vent is formed. Stitch centre back seam as far as the top of the vent pressing the seam open and the vent towards the left back. Attach side back to back, stitch seams, clip curves and press open and then interface. The two back neck darts will be included in the interfacing but these should not be stitched in the normal manner but slashed open, the edges lapped and stitched and thereafter the excess

134

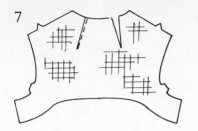

7

8

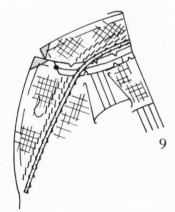

9

fabric can be trimmed away (diagram 7). Machine baste the interfacing $\frac{1}{2}$ inch from the neck edge, armholes and side seams and trim close to this point. You are now ready to start forming the garment so stitch the shoulder seams and side seams and then try the garment on for fitting. It is important to remember that you have still to insert a lining so the garment should not be fitted too tightly.

Collar Attach the collar canvas to the wrong side of the under collar and baste in position $\frac{1}{2}$ inch from the raw edges. Then, with the right side of the under collar, to the right side of the garment, pin along seam line matching all construction symbols and baste. At this point the jacket must either be fitted on you by another person or you will need a dressmaker's dummy to enable you to do it yourself. It is now important to establish a roll line for the collar and lapels (diagram 8). Put the garment on the dress-stand and matching the centres, pin the buttonhole across to the corresponding button placement and then you can set the collar and the front lapels such that they roll to form a smooth line. Using tailor's chalk, mark in this roll line on the collar and the lapels and remove the garment from the stand. The under collar should now be removed from the garment and the roll line of the collar and lapels held with a length of twill tape or straight seam binding. The tape is laid with one edge running alongside the roll line and the remainder of the tape extending towards the garment. Hand sew the tape to the garment along both long edges with blind stitches through the interfacing picking-up only a thread from the garment fabric so that the stitches will not show through on the right side of the garment (diagram 9).

Pad stitching The lapels are now ready for pad stitching and this is the beginning of the moulding process which gives the garment extra body and shape. Pad stitching is worked from the wrong side of the garment and used to hold the interfacing to the garment fabric. Hold the fabric in your left hand rolling the work over it as you stitch (diagram 10). Take stitches from right to left about $\frac{1}{4}$–$\frac{3}{8}$ inch long through the interfacing picking-up only a thread from the garment fabric so that the

10

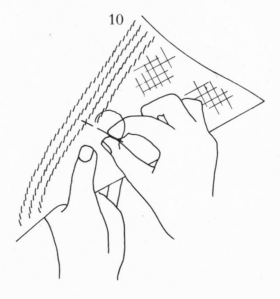

stitches will not show through on the right side. Each stitch should be approximately half an inch below the previous one such that the stitches form diagonally. Work the stitching lines from the top of the lapel downwards forming parallel lines at half inch intervals. When the pad stitching is completed the lapel should be steam pressed over a tailor's ham.

Holding the collar in your left hand, take stitches from left to right about $\frac{1}{4}-\frac{3}{8}$ inch in length through the interfacing itself picking-up only a thread or two from the actual garment fabric. Each stitch is placed approximately $\frac{1}{2}$ inch below the other and in this way a row of slanting stitches is formed. Make parallel rows of pad stitching to the first always holding the collar in your left hand and forming the shape by rolling the collar over your fingers as you stitch. Pad stitch to within $\frac{1}{2}$ inch of the raw edges and then when you have completed your stitching towards the neck edge, start from the roll line again making your lines of stitching further apart this time and working towards the collar points. Trim the interfacing up to the pad stitching.

The under collar can now be attached to the neck edge of the jacket. This process may be made easier provided the neck edge has first of all been stay stitched, by clipping into the seam allowance up to the stay stitching and then stitching the collar to the neck edge to the point where the collar joins the lapel. Press the seam open over a tailor's ham and then hang the garment up whilst you prepare the upper collar and facing.

Front facing and upper collar Stitch front facing to back neck facing at shoulder seams and then with the right sides together, attach the upper collar to the neck edge of the facing up to the construction symbol denoting the break between the collar and the lapel. It is most important that you do not stitch beyond this point so secure thread ends in the exact position (diagram 11). Seam turnings should then be trimmed and clipped and pressed open over a tailor's ham. You are now ready to attach this unit to the garment so with right sides together pin the facing and the upper collar to the jacket lapel and the under collar matching all the construction symbols very accurately.

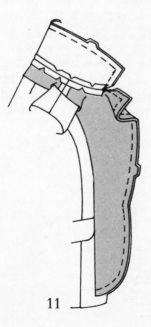

11

It is advisable to baste along the seam line first and follow the basting line accurately when stitching. Trim the seam allowance and corners and clip all curves before turning the facing and upper collar through to the inside. Use a pair of closed scissors again to help you push out the points of the lapels and collar and then, matching the neck seams, from the inside, tack the lower seam turnings of the neck edge together loosely.

Hem On a tailored garment, the hem is not taken-up on to the garment fabric itself but on to interfacing. The interfacing should be cut on the true bias and should measure the hem depth plus 1 inch. Half an inch of this will extend above the finished hem and $\frac{1}{2}$ inch below the fold line of the hem to prevent the interfacing from forming too hard an edge. Baste the interfacing in position so that it just laps the front interfacing and runs from this point to the fold line of the jacket vent. Hold in position with long running stitches taking up only a thread from the garment with each stitch and then turn the hem up the required amount. The left back vent extension is pressed back to the inside along the fold line which will be an extension of the centre back stitching line and on the right back vent extension press under the $\frac{5}{8}$ inch seam allowance. Actually sewing up the hem is a joy to those who hate doing small hemming stitches because the hem is held to the interfacing with long running stitches. Afterwards the facings can be catch-stitched to the hem at the lower edge and the left back vent is also catch-stitched to the hem at the lower edge.

If you wanted to add a finishing touch to the jacket in the form of top-stitching the collar and the lapels, this would be the moment to do it.

Sleeves A tailored garment does not have darts in the sleeves but the sleeve is formed in two pieces so that one part can be eased on to the other providing the necessary ease or room for movement. Stitch the seams of the sleeve and then attach the interfacing to the lower edge in the same way as you did with the lower edge of the garment. Cut the interfacing an inch wider than the hem depth (diagram 12), attach in position with catch or long running stitches and then turn up the hem on to the interfacing and hold to the interfacing, again with long running stitches (diagram 13). The sleeve is now ready to insert into the armhole of the jacket and this can be done by making two rows of machine stitches around the sleeve head between the notches. However, it is quite possible to insert the sleeve without going through this process. With the garment wrong side out and the sleeve right side out, drop the sleeve through the armhole and then insert six pins to hold the sleeve in the correct position.

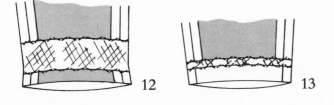

12   13

A well-tailored jacket goes anywhere

Turning the seam turnings over your left hand, pin the sleeve to the armhole, easing in the fullness. Baste and try jacket on to check the sleeve positioning. Sleeve can then be removed from armhole and with ease stitches held firm, fit the sleeve head over a tailor's ham and steam press to shrink out fullness (diagram 14). Leave over the ham until quite dry then re-fit the sleeve into armhole. Baste and stitch $\frac{5}{8}$ inch from the raw edges and then make a further line of machine stitching of $\frac{1}{8}$ inch from this towards the raw edges. Trim the seam turnings below the notches and press the sleeve turnings only as you did with your previous set in sleeve.

14

Finishing From the right side the garment will now appear complete. However, on the wrong side slash the facing to neaten the rear side of the bound buttonhole and to sew the button in position on the left front. The button will need to be sewn on a shank to prevent it from pulling the buttonhole. The shank may be incorporated into the button itself or may have to be worked with thread. Having first of all taken a small stitch in the fabric to secure the thread end, bring the needle and thread up through the button then place a matchstick across the top of the button before inserting the needle through the other side of the button and down through the fabric (diagram 15). Keep the stick in position until the button is secure and then remove it. The button will now be loose with a space between button and the fabric. Wind the thread around the button threads thus forming a shank (diagram 16). Fasten the thread end off tightly.

15   16

Lining The pattern instruction sheet will contain special notes with regard to cutting out the pattern pieces for the lining. The notes will normally be situated in the cutting layouts for the jacket lining. For instance if pattern pieces for the jacket are used to cut the lining as well, they will probably require shortening. It is also necessary to add 1 inch at the back neck tapering off to nothing at the lower edge by placing the back lining pattern piece of grain by $\frac{1}{2}$ inch at the back neck. This is known as a pleat allowance which is later stitched down for 1 to 2 inches releasing extra fabric into the jacket lining for extra room for movement. This serves the purpose of helping to prevent the lining from ripping at the armhole.

The most difficult part about lining a jacket is cutting the lining so that it fits the back vent. Once this is accomplished the remainder is quickly and easily stitched into place. First, lay the two back lining pieces in front of you right sides down

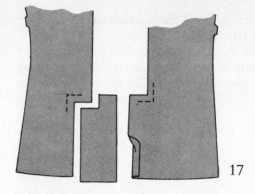

17

onto the table with the centre back edges towards the centre (diagram 17). Start with the piece of lining on your left and trim away the vent extension as shown. Reinforce the corner and then clip into the corner up to the stitching line. You will then be able to press the $\frac{5}{8}$ inch seam turnings towards the wrong side so that the left portion is complete. For the section of lining to your right, reinforce the corner and then clip into the corner up to the stitching line. Press under the $\frac{5}{8}$ inch seam turning along the back edge of the extension. Now stitch the centre back seam as far as the vent construction symbol and then form the pleat by stitching down from the neck edge for 2 inches $\frac{1}{2}$ inch inside the centre back seam and secure thread ends (diagram 18). This is the pleat extension formed. Make sure that you do not trim away the wrong piece of back lining. Follow the instructions carefully and then stitch the side back to the back, clipping seams and pressing the seam turnings open. A separate lining pattern piece will always be included for the front of the jacket which will have a tuck from the shoulder seam again to introduce a little extra fullness to allow the necessary ease of movement (diagram 19). Stitch the dart and

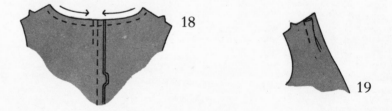

18

19

the tuck in position and press towards the centre front and then at the side and shoulder seams join the front to the back.

Inserting the lining Turn your jacket completely inside out and place on the dressmaker's dummy. The lining has a $\frac{5}{8}$ inch seam allowance all round which can be pressed to the wrong side provided this is done with extreme caution to prevent stretching. Now slip the lining right side out over your jacket passing the jacket sleeve through the armholes of the lining. Match all construction symbols, shoulder seams, side seams and centre back seams. Slip stitch the lining to the facings by hand (diagram 20). Baste the armhole seam turnings together close to the stitching line and slip stitch the lining down onto the back vent. The hem allowance should be turned up on the lining and turn-

20

ing the fold of the lining back about ¼ inch, catch the hem of the lining to the hem of the garment.

Inserting sleeve linings Form the seams in the sleeve linings as for the jacket sleeves and baste around the sleeve head, turning under the ⅝ inch seam turning all round. Clip the seam turning at the underarm and cut small notches out around the sleeve head. Pin the lining with the folded edge just covering the seam line and then slip stitch into position taking care to match construction symbols (diagram 21). Take up the lining hem in the same manner as for the lower edge of the jacket and the garment is complete. If, when you try on the jacket, you find that it could be helped by a little weight at the lower edge, sew in a chain weight between the lining hem and the jacket hem and tucked out of sight underneath the fold of the lining.

21

Coat

Once a satisfactory finish on a tailored jacket is mastered, dressmaking will give you no problems in the future. You may think a coat is way beyond your capabilities but in fact a coat is more simple to sew. A lot of the sewing processes are the same and the lining should again be sewn in by hand rather than by machine for the best finish. A couturier does not sew any seams on a lining by machine but overlays each seam onto the other and holds them together with hand stitches. This is therefore the best method of all. A swing tack is used to hold a loose lining to the garment usually at the side seam. A quick method has already been described but this method is stronger for use in coats. Secure the thread end and then take a small stitch in the hem of the garment and (in the hem of the lining leaving a thread approximately 1 inch between them. Repeat 2 or 3 times then blanket stitch over the threads between the two pieces of fabric) and neaten the thread end.

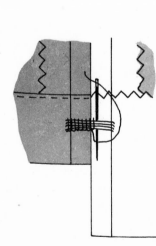

If you decide to sew a coat the only process that you are likely to encounter which has not already been covered is the formation of a pocket in a seam.

Pocket in a seam Pockets can be inserted into a side seam or into a side front seam and this type of pocket is quickly and easily formed. For each pocket you will have two pieces of fabric; the garment will probably have extensions to the seam turning to which the pocket should be attached. With the right sides of the fabric together and carefully matching the construction symbols, stitch one side of the pocket to one seam extension and the other side of the pocket to the other seam extension (diagram 22). Trim the seams and press them open. Next, form the seam in the garment by placing the fabric right sides together and stitch as far as the pocket markings before pivoting machine and stitching round the two pocket pieces placed right sides together (diagram 23). Pivot machine again and stitch seam to lower edge. Clip seam allowance of back section of pocket.

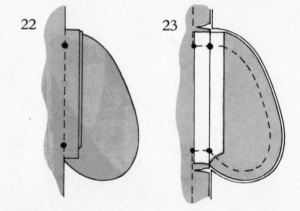

Press seams open above and below pocket. Press the pocket towards the front of the garment lightly from the wrong side then turning the work over to the right side press again forming a neat fold on the front section from the right side.

A wraparound is a popular design and the front is held closed with a tie belt which is formed in the same way as the shirt dress belt. Alternatively, a stiff interfaced belt can be made and attached to a purchased buckle. Use commercial belting to interface and stiffen the belt. This can be bought in a variety of widths and cut to the length of your waist measurement plus 6 inches. At one end of the stiffening cut a right angled point (diagram 24). Prepare a strip of fabric twice the width of the belt stiffening plus $\frac{3}{4}$ inch and the length of the stiffening plus $\frac{3}{4}$ inch. Turn under $\frac{1}{4}$ inch along one of the long edges and stitch. The fabric should now be folded lengthways right sides together with the stitched edge $\frac{1}{4}$ inch from the other raw edge. Pin and stitch a $\frac{1}{4}$ inch seam and trim the corner. The fabric can now be unfolded and refolded so that this seam line follows the line of the first fold (diagram 25). Press seam open then turn the fabric through so that the right sides are outside. Insert the belt stiffening into this formed point and then fold up the raw edge over the stiffening and press. Fold over the finished edge, encasing the raw edge and slip stitch (diagram 26). Press care-

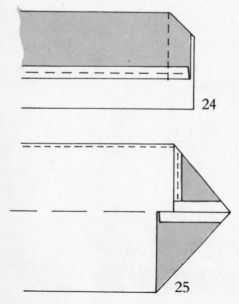

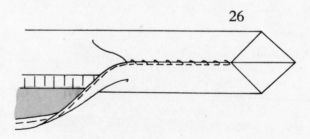

Bold checks teamed with tailoring detail

143

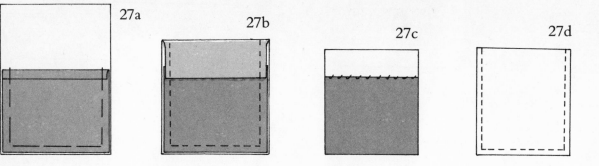

fully and then you are ready to attach it to the buckle. Fold the other unfinished edge of the belt over the centre bar to the wrong side of the belt and then turning under the raw edge, sew in position by hand making sure that the stitches are firm.

Lined patch pocket Press under $\frac{5}{8}$ inch seam allowance at the top of the pocket lining (diagram 27a). Baste to pocket with right sides together. Fold pocket along fold line as indicated and stitch along lower edge and the two sides (diagram 27b). Trim seam turnings, clip corners and turn through (diagram 27c). Slip-stitch lining in position. Pocket can now be topstitched into position on right side of garment (diagram 27d).

Braid trim A popular method of personalising a simple coat design such as the wraparound coat is to apply a braid trim around the edges of the garment. This is easily done by top stitching the braid into position but the braid will need to be mitred at the corners. Pin the braid in position down as far as the corner and then top stitch in position stitching close to both edges of the braid, finishing the stitching at the lower edge. Fold the braid straight back on itself at the lower edge. Press the fold before refolding the trim, forming a pleat in the braid so that it will lie along the other edge (diagram 28). This will form a diagonal crease in the braid. Lift the braid and top stitch along the diagonal crease through two thicknesses of braid and through to the wrong side of the garment. Replace braid and recommence top stitching close to both edges from the diagonal seam line (diagram 29).

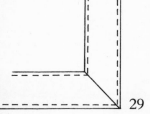

68

71

72

84

85

91

92

93

FAMILY CIRCLE

By now you will probably be a fairly self-assured dressmaker and will feel that you could extend your capabilities to make clothes for other members of your family. Why not let the man in your life show off your sewing capabilities for you?

Whether you plan to sew for a young boy, teenage boy or fully grown man the body measurements should be taken with care and compared with the manufacturer's sizing charts. From this you will quickly determine the correct pattern size to use.

Measurement chart for men and boys

Body measurement	Where to measure	Your measurements
Height	Measure height without shoes, from the floor to the top of the head	
Chest	Around the fullest part of the chest	
Waist	Around the natural waistline	
Hip	Measure around the fullest part of the hips about 9 inches below the waist	
Neck	Measure neck and add $\frac{1}{2}$ inch to determine collar size. This should be comparable to the neck size of your ready-to-wear shirts	
Sleeve length	From shoulder point over bent elbow to wrist	
Inside Leg	Measure from the crutch down the inside leg seam to the desired finished length	
Side waist length	Measure from the side of the waist over hip down outside trouser side seam to desired finished length	

Pattern manufacturers' catalogues show boy's and men's patterns in a separate section to make the process of selection simpler. A shirt is one of the garments in which a man is most

161

able to show his personality. As you have already mastered a shirt dress for yourself, this would seem a sensible place to start. Most of the sewing processes are very similar.

Man's shirt

One of the most off-putting things about these patterns is that they often seem to contain so many different pattern pieces. This is usually because several views of one shirt will be included in the pattern. Select the pattern pieces you require and you will find that this can be as few as seven – front, back, yoke, collar, collar-stay, sleeve and cuff. The pattern may also include an optional patch pocket.

Make the pleats in the back of the shirt. These normally face out towards the arm holes. The front facing is cut in one with the shirt. Cut two strips of interfacing the length of the front facing and the width as recommended by the pattern manufacturer (usually $2\frac{1}{4}$ inches to $2\frac{1}{2}$ inches). On the wrong side of the facing, iron on interfacing with one edge running along the fold line and the other towards the raw edge. Neaten the raw edge by turning it to wrong side and edge stitching. Fold the interfaced section back to the wrong side of the front. Baste firmly in position along the fold line.

Yoke You will have noted, when cutting out, that it was necessary to cut two yokes. One of the peculiarities of a man's shirt is that they always have a faced yoke. Encase the shirt back between the right sides of the two yokes (diagram 1). Stitch the seam through all three thicknesses, trim and press both yokes away from the shirt back. Attach right side of under yoke to wrong side of the shirt front. Pin and stitch seam. Trim turnings and press away from the shirt front onto the yoke. Along the corresponding edge of the upper yoke, press under the $\frac{5}{8}$ inch seam turning, trim. Overlay the fold onto the stitching line, baste and edge stitch close to the fold (diagram 2). Topstitch

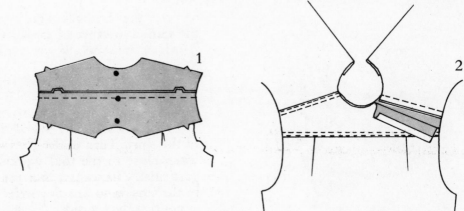

$\frac{1}{4}$ inch from this and repeat the process along the back yoke seam.
Collar You will have cut one piece of interfacing for the collar itself and another piece of interfacing for the collar stay. The collar pattern piece incorporates the neck band and the collar stay is used to provide extra stiffening for the neck band. Two pieces of fabric have been cut out for the collar; the upper collar and the under collar. Iron interfacing into position (diagram 3). Iron collar stay into position over the interfacing on the wrong side of the under collar (diagram 4). Stitch upper and under

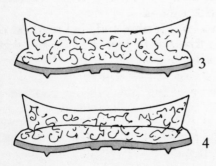

collars together as the neck seam allowance. Turn the collar through gently pushing out the points with a pair of closed scissors and then press. With right sides together attach under collar to shirt along neck edge. Trim turnings, clip curve and press turnings towards collar. On the upper collar press under the $\frac{5}{8}$ inch seam turnings and trim to $\frac{1}{4}$ inch. Bring fold down over line of stitching and slip stitch from the wrong side of the garment (diagram 5). Topstitch collar $\frac{1}{4}$ inch from finished edge as indicated.

Sleeve opening Most men's shirt patterns neaten the sleeve opening by the continuous strip method used on the shirt dress. However, always follow your pattern instruction sheet carefully as it will recommend the best method for the cuff you are using. The lower edge of the sleeve is pleated into the cuff rather than gathered (diagram 6). There are not normally more than two pleats.

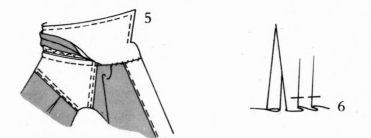

Inserting the sleeve Because the armhole seam is to be double stitched it is easier to insert the sleeve before the side seams and the under-arm sleeve seams are stitched. With the right sides together, pin the sleeve into the armhole. Stitch the armhole seam $\frac{5}{8}$ inch from the raw edges. Leaving the sleeve seam allowance at $\frac{5}{8}$ inch, trim the armhole seam allowance to $\frac{1}{4}$ inch and clip as necessary. Press both seam turnings away from the sleeve towards the shirt and make a double stitched seam by lapping the seam allowance of the sleeve onto the shirt, turning under $\frac{1}{4}$ inch of the seam allowance and then edge stitching (diagram 7).

Seams With the right sides together, pin and stitch the side seam continuing into the under arm sleeve seam. Reduce the seam turning of the back of the shirt to $\frac{1}{4}$ inch continuing through on the sleeve seam. Press both seam turnings towards the back of the shirt. Turn under $\frac{1}{4}$ inch of the seam turning and edge stitch close to the fold working from the wrong side. (It is particularly important that your machine is correctly adjusted to the tension so that the under side of your stitching will look as good as the top side). Neaten the lower edge of the back and front shirt with a narrow stitched hem.

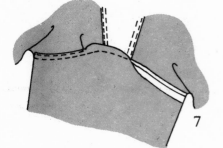

Cuff Unless the pattern includes a double cuff, the method of working will be identical to that which was used on the shirt dress cuff. After the cuff has been attached to the sleeve, top stitch $\frac{1}{4}$ inch from all finished edges as indicated.

Buttons and buttonholes Make machine buttonholes and when these are complete and cut open, sew buttons in position. Remember that you are now making a man's shirt and, therefore, the buttonholes will be formed in the left front and the buttons sewn onto the right front.

163

Man's trousers

It will be necessary to master the insertion of a proper fly-zip, back welt pockets and side front pockets. The waist band is attached in a similar way though it is seamed in a slightly different manner at centre back and afterwards belt carriers are attached.

Fly front zipper A separate pattern piece is included for the fly and this is cut out from double thickness fabric. The left fly is interfaced, and stitched to the left trouser front (diagram 8). Trouser front will already have been reinforced between the notches enabling you to clip into the stitching line and then trim away the seam turnings above this point to $\frac{1}{4}$ inch. Open out the fly, pressing seam turnings towards fly. Place a closed zipper face down with the lower end about $\frac{1}{4}$ inch above the construction symbol (diagram 9). The edge of the right hand zipper tape should run along the fly seam line and then the left hand zipper tape stitched to the fly using a zipper foot. Run one line of machine stitching close to the zipper teeth with a further line of stitching a $\frac{1}{4}$ inch from this. Press the fly to the inside of the garment, baste into position along the seam line being careful not to catch in the lower part of the right hand zipper tape. Top stitch (diagram 10). On the right trouser front clip as indicated and press under the seam turning, above this point. Open the zipper and then pin the right front over the zipper tape as close to the teeth as possible (diagram 11). The left front should now lap the right front by $\frac{1}{4}$ inch with the two construction symbols matching (diagram 12). Baste in position and then form the right fly. Baste in position and then top stitch through all thicknesses using a zipper foot to enable you to stitch closely to the zipper teeth.

The fly zipper fastening is now complete leaving the lower portion of the crotch seam to be stitched later.

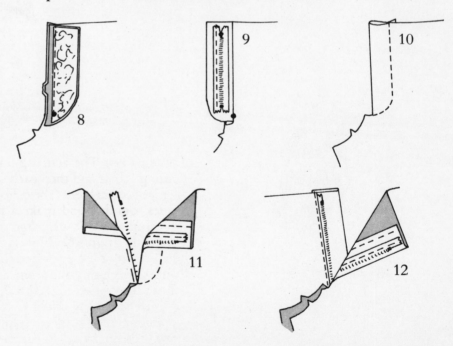

Welt pockets These are the slit-like pockets which are usually worked in the back of men's trousers. The method of working is very similar to that used for forming the welt pocket with

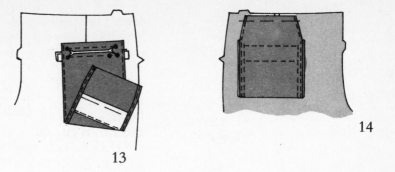

14

13

flap on the jacket. Fold the welt in half lengthwise and baste in position. The back pocket has a facing cut from garment fabric which is attached to the pocket as indicated. With the right sides together, baste the pocket along the pocket line over the welt matching the construction symbols (diagram 13). Stitch along stitching lines but do not stitch across the ends. Slash as for a bound button hole first on the pocket and then on the garment itself. Take care not to cut the ends of the welt. Turn the pocket through the slashed opening to the wrong side. Sew the small triangles to the welt. Fold pocket up on fold line and pin and stitch the side edges together (diagram 14). Stitch side edges along seam line below upper edge of pocket catching in the triangles. With the right side of the trouser back towards you, turn the waist line edge of the trousers down and then pin and stitch the pocket to the seam turnings, to hold the back part of the pocket steady (diagram 15). Baste the upper edge of the pocket to the waistline edge of the trousers.

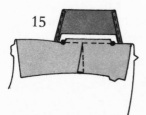

15

16

Side pockets The actual pocket pattern piece will be cut out of lining fabric and then each side of the pocket will be faced with a piece of garment fabric. Fold the pocket in half with the wrong sides together and make a French seam from the construction symbol at the lower edge of the pocket opening round to the fold (diagram 16). Now with the right sides together pin the front part of the pocket to the front opening edge of the trousers and stitch along the seam line to the waist edge (diagram 17). Turn the pocket to the inside and then press before top stitching $\frac{1}{4}$ inch from the stitched edge. Stitch pocket to back trouser opening edge and press the seam open, turning the pocket towards the front. Bring the front edge of the pocket to match the construction symbol on the pocket back and pin (diagram 18). Baste the upper edges of the pocket to the front trouser at the seam line.

17

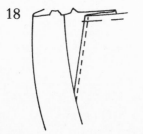

18

Waist band The waist band is attached in two sections, i.e., the left side to the trouser left side and the right side to the trouser right side.

Pin the crotch seam starting at the lower end of the fly opening with the right sides together matching the inside leg seams and stitching through to the upper end of the waist band (diagram 19). Trim the seam and clip the curves then press the seam turnings open above the last clip. Turn under the upper edges of the waist band and hem down onto the inside of the waist band. This is a useful method of finishing men's trousers because it helps to achieve good fit.

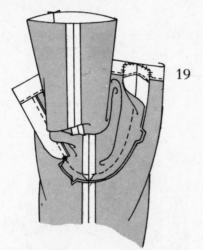

19

Belt carriers Cut strips of fabric from garment remnants $1\frac{1}{4}$ inches wide and $3\frac{1}{2}$ inches long. The length may be varied according to the width of the waist band and the width of the belt which they are to carry. They may also be formed in one continuous strip and cut up later. Press under $\frac{1}{4}$ inch on the long edges of the strip then fold the strip in half lengthwise with the wrong sides to the centre. Machine stitch close to both edges. On the outside of the trousers, attach the lower edge of the belt carrier to the trouser fabric just below the waist band. Stitch a $\frac{1}{4}$ inch from the raw edge then fold the carrier over the line of stitching bringing it up over the top of the waist band securing the remaining end by a $\frac{1}{4}$ inch on the under side or wrong side of the waist band.

Sewing with suede and leather

Sewing suedes and leather can be a source of enormous enjoyment and because these materials do not fray, they are almost easier to sew than fabric. A few basic sewing techniques must be learned so that you know how to reduce bulk but from there on it really is easy.

The right pattern Pattern manufacturers produce a limited number of patterns which are specifically for suedes and leathers. However, other designs can quite easily be adapted. It may be necessary sometimes to add in a horizontal seam or a yoke in which case remember to add seam turnings. A panelled design is often a good choice because the skins can be used to good advantage when cutting-out. The size of the skins must impose certain limitations by their length and shape but an excellent garment on which to make a start would be a sleeveless waistcoat or a skirt.

How many skins to use Skins are supplied by the square foot and

Trousers finished with a belt carrier

the skins from a sheep vary between 5 and 8 square feet whereas larger calf skins measure between 12 and 17 square feet. On the whole, suppliers are enormously helpful regarding calculations as to how many skins are required. If you have selected a pattern which specifies leather or suede, it will usually state the square footage required and the type of skin to use.

Special sewing equipment You will require special needles (spear-point) for your sewing machine and special glover's needles for hand sewing. Synthetic threads are ideal because they are strong and provide elasticity to match up with the stretch in the skin. A ballpoint pen is used to transfer construction symbols, and a stapling machine together with a staple remover, a tube or pot of fabric adhesive and clear adhesive tape will also be necessary.

Cutting If your pattern is not specifically designed for suedes and leathers, trim seam turnings to $\frac{3}{8}$ inch all round. Suede has a nap or pile and, therefore, all pattern pieces should run in the same direction. All possible pattern adaptations should be completed at this stage to prevent difficulties later.

Fittings Because leather punctures as you stitch, you should never back stitch or restitch a seam because this can cut the skin. Fit the garment prior to stitching. Match the appropriate seam lines and hold together with staples. This will not hold the garment firmly in place but will act as a guide so that you can make minor fitting alterations.

Stitching Use a machine stitch length of about 8 to 10 stitches to the inch and stitch along seam lines slowly remembering that your seam allowance has been reduced. If you are sewing on very fine suede, run a strip of tissue paper along the seam line between the under layer of suede and the machine itself to prevent the feed teeth on the machine from damaging the skin. The tissue can easily be torn away after stitching.

Seams can be made in the usual manner and the seam turnings glued back. If the skin is stiff, it may be necessary to use your pounding block to flatten the seams. Darts are also stitched in the same way but are then cut open, trimmed and glued open. Clip the outer edges of curves and cut small notches on the inside edges of curves before glueing into position.

Facings Facings can be omitted altogether in which case the seam allowance is clipped and then glued back to the wrong side of the garment folding on the seam line. However, it is usually advisable to face armholes, etc., for more lasting finish in which case after the process just described is completed, trim the seam allowance on the facing as far as the seam line. With the wrong side of the facing to the wrong side of the garment simply place the seam line of the facing up to the folded edge of the garment and glue. You can then top stitch from the right side of garment through all thicknesses.

Hems Hem edges can be left raw but look neater if glued up into position and hammered lightly or top stitched from the right side $\frac{1}{2}$ inch to $\frac{3}{4}$ inch from the folded edge.

Sleeves It is perfectly possible to set in sleeves in the usual manner but if difficulty is encountered, you may find it easier to hand sew the arm hole seam with firm back stitches rather than using the machine. The ease in the sleeve head can be reduced but this is not advisable because it will place extra strain on the arm hole seam which may cause it to tear later.

Zipper Stitch the seam as far as the zip opening and glue back the seam turnings above and below this point. Working from the side of the garment place the zipper face down with the zipper teeth over the zipper opening and then hold in position with clear adhesive tape on the wrong side of the garment. Stitch from the right side and then tear away the adhesive tape when the stitching is completed. Bound button holes can be made very successfully on suede and leather by the piped method.

Finishing details As an alternative to top stitching from the right side, saddle stitching gives a marvellous hand finished look. It is worked like running stitches with the stitches and the spaces between them measuring approximately $\frac{1}{4}$ inch. To press a suede or leather garment, use a dry iron on a warm setting and press over brown paper. When you have finished your garment keep the remnant pieces because these can be cut up to make applique shapes for future garments.

Sewing for children
Dress making for children can be easy and fun and is sometimes the way in which women gain their first introduction to sewing. First take body measurements to select correct pattern size.

Measurement chart for children

Body measurement	Where to measure	Your measurements
Height	Without shoes from floor to top of the head	
Chest	Across shoulder blades, high under the arms and round fullest part of chest	
Waist	At natural waistline	
Hips	Round fullest part	
Back waist length	From neck to waist at centre back	
Skirt length	From natural waistline to desired hem length	
Trouser length	From waist to desired length at side seam	

For babies, it is necessary to know the age, weight and length. As soon as a baby becomes a toddler, the measurements are the same as those which you took to determine your own pattern size. A chart is included so that you may record the measurements in pencil. If it is some time since you last sewed a garment for your child, be sure to check the measurements again in case they have changed.

When selecting the appropriate pattern type and size, remember that the size categories bear no relevance to age at all so select your pattern size by the body measurements. Through sewing, you are able to provide your child with a much better fit simply as a result of the different sizing categories that are available rather than having to choose a dress from a dress-rail in a shop marked 'age 4'.

Most of the sewing processes used for making children's clothes have already been covered in the previous chapters, but many people feel inspired to embroider or trim children's clothes, so a variety of trimming methods are included. These could be adapted for use on your own clothes too.

Children's clothes are usually designed so that they will either be simple and very quick to sew or fun to sew, incorporating decorative details such as smocking. A design is featured here which would in fact be suitable for a girl from toddler age group through to a teenager. You will notice that instead of having a cuff at the lower edge of the sleeve, the fullness in the sleeve is simply taken in to an elastic casing.

An elastic casing This finish can be used for full sleeves in a variety of lengths and provides a simple quick method of forming a fashion sleeve. Stitch underarm sleeve seam and press $\frac{1}{4}$ inch at the lower edge of the sleeve to the wrong side and then turn up the lower folded edge to form a hem slightly wider than the elastic (diagram 20). Your pattern instruction sheet will always quote accurate measurements for the design. Machine stitch close to the edge of the hem and leave an opening at the underarm seam 1–$1\frac{1}{2}$ inches wide. Thread the elastic through the casing, using a safety pin firmly pinned to one end whilst the other end remains pinned to the seam turning. Lap the ends of the elastic and test for fit before sewing together either by hand or machine (diagram 21). Tuck the elastic inside the casing and close the opening with machine stitches.

20

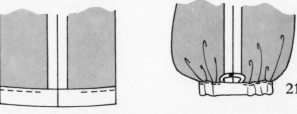

21

Detachable collar The Peter Pan collar illustrated here is a popular design detail for children's and adult's clothes. If a collar is to be of a light colour, it is always advisable to have it detachable and on children's clothes, by making a detachable collar, it is possible to ring the changes with different shapes and contrasting and toning colours. The method for forming the unit can be directly applied for cuffs as well. Form the collar in the usual way. Press firmly and tack the neck edges together along the seam line, trimming the seam turnings to $\frac{1}{4}$ inch. The raw edges now require binding either with ready-made bias seam binding or with a bias strip of lining fabric (diagram 22). Bind the raw edges inside the bias strip turning in the ends and edge stitch close to the folded edges through all thicknesses. The collar can be attached to the dress with basting stitches worked on the wrong side of the garment which must be unpicked when it is removed for cleaning or washing. Alternatively, snap fasteners or a touch and close fastener can be sewn on at intervals to the collar and the garment. Make sure that you carefully match the collar to the neck edge for accurate positioning of the snap fasteners and in this way you can make sure that the collar is truly detachable for easy care.

Detachable collars and cuffs are an excellent way to transform a basic shift with long fitted sleeves into an attractive party dress. The basic dress can be made in a cotton needlecord in a bright colour such as red or emerald green and trimmed with a white piqué collar and cuffs.

Shirring Machine shirring is better for children's clothes. The machine is threaded with the appropriate thread on the top of the machine and the bobbin is wound with shirring elastic.

22

170

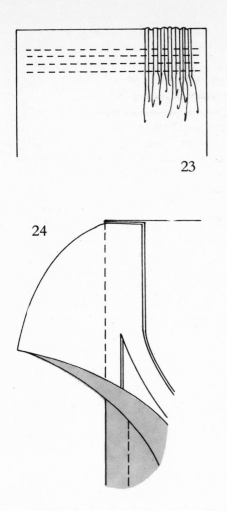

23

24

Make the requisite number of rows of machine stitching across the fabric, setting the machine for a basting stitch (diagram 23). The fabric will gather up as you stitch but should be straightened as you stitch the next row. Leave the thread ends a good length on each row to be fastened off later. This will ensure even stitches, save considerable time and elasticize the gathers for a truly comfortable fit.

French seam The usual $\frac{5}{8}$ inch seam allowance is allowed when cutting-out. Each seam is placed wrong sides together and then stitched $\frac{3}{8}$ inch from the raw edges. Press the seams as stitched, then press the seam allowances over to one side. Trim seam allowances to $\frac{1}{8}$ inch and then turning the fabric right sides together, fold along previous stitching line and press (diagram 24). A line of stitching is now made on the seam line to enclose the raw edges. This type of seam is commonly used for children's clothes and for fine and sheer fabrics.

Hand worked button hole Fine fabrics often respond better to hand worked rather than machine button holes. As with machine button holes, these are worked after the garment is completed.

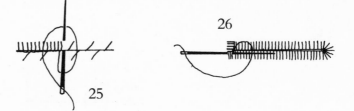

26

25

Mark the button holes in exactly the same manner. Using sharp scissors, slash the length of the button hole which should be the diameter of the button plus $\frac{1}{8}$ inch. Follow grain of the fabric to help you cut a straight line. Over sew the cut edges with small stitches and then making sure that you have threaded your needle with sufficient thread to complete the button hole, work button hole stitches from left to right along its length (diagram 25). Insert the needle through the slit bringing it out below the over-sewing and loop the thread from the needle eye under the point of the needle from right to left. Pull the needle through so that the thread forms a small knot on top of the cut edge. Work the stitches at an even distance from each other so that the knots cover the raw edge. The length of the stitches should be $\frac{1}{16}$–$\frac{1}{8}$ inch long. At the garment end edge, form a fan of stitches, keeping the centre stitch in line with the slit. Turn the work and continue stitching along the top edge. Make a bar at the opposite end by first taking two or three stitches across the end and then working blanket stitches over the threads and through the garment fabric (diagram 26).

Tucks Tucks are formed in groups and must be exactly the same width with the space between the tucks carefully measured. When tucks are made by hand, either follow the markings on the pattern tissue or cut a measuring gauge. A straight piece of cardboard can be notched to help form tucks accurately and the time taken to form the cardboard will soon be made up when making the tucks. Cut one notch in the card the depth of the finished tuck and another to mark the distance between them measuring from one stitching line to the next.

For hand sewn tucks, fold the edge for the tuck and then sew it with a fine running stitch, using a fine needle and thread.

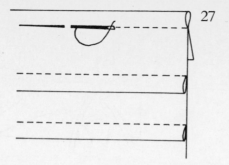

27

Secure thread ends firmly (diagram 27). It is usual to form tucks by hand on very fine or sheer fabrics. On heavier fabrics tucks can be stitched by machine measuring and spacing in exactly the same manner.

Pin tucks These are used as decoration on very sheer fabrics and on children's and babies' clothes. The tuck is stitched by hand so that it is only $\frac{1}{16}$ inch wide.

Machine-corded tucks On most zig-zag machines it is possible to run tucks encasing a cord. The manufacturer's instruction booklet will give you exact instructions but the principle is that you usually use a twin needle and feed the cord through the bed of the machine up into the underside of the work (diagram 28). With the right side of the work uppermost, the machine forms twin lines of stitching and feeds the cord between them to give a raised effect. This is a quick and easy method of forming tucks which last well and can be done on light to medium weight fabrics.

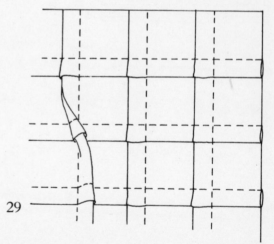

29

Cross tucks These are sometimes used for decoration on yokes or sometimes all over blouses which are made from see through fabrics. First of all, make hand tucks marking and stitching all the tucks on the lengthwise grain and pressing them in one direction. Keeping the depth of the tucks the same and the measurement between them the same, mark the tucks horizontally on the crosswise grain, stitch and again press in the same direction (diagram 29).

Hems If you are in a hurry to complete a hem, you might like to consider using a bonding material such as a fuseable fleece. This is a method of joining one fabric layer to another which is used for applying appliqués and can also be used for taking-up hems. The bonding materials are carefully manufactured and tested and are sold with instructions as to how to press them to obtain

172

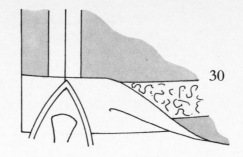

30

the best results. Always read the manufacturer's instructions carefully. The bonding materials which are paper backed, can be cut to any shape and for a hem should be placed paper side up on the wrong side of the hem and pressed firmly with a dry iron (diagram 30). Allow it to cool and then peel the paper away. You can then turn up the hem and press it to the garment using a press cloth and a steam iron. The bonding material should then adhere firmly to both pieces of fabric holding the hem in position. Bonding materials are also available in narrow strips and not backed with any paper. Cut the strips to the desired length and place between the two layers of fabric. Press firmly according to the manufacturer's instructions and the two surfaces should adhere. Make sure that the iron does not touch the bonding material, otherwise, these two surfaces will cling together and the base of your iron will be difficult to clean.

Ruffles Ruffles can be formed in a variety of ways to provide a decorative and feminine finish to a variety of garments and household items. Those that are cut on the bias will form softer folds but a variety of attractive trimming effects can be achieved with the various types.

Ruffles to trim a cuff Purchased ruffles of lace or broderie anglais can be inserted into the seams of collars, cuffs or even panelling seams of blouses. The gathers will already have been drawn up for you so before the seam is sewn, baste the ruffle to the right side of the fabric along one seam edge with the ruffle facing in towards the garment and the edges facing in the same direction as the raw edges (diagram 31). Place the facing piece of fabric over the right sides together and then stitch along the seam line through all thicknesses (diagram 32). Trim the seam turnings, corners and turn through to the right side before pressing (diagram 33).

Single ruffle A strip of fabric is cut to the required length and width on the lengthwise, crosswise or bias grain and one of the long raw edges neatened by turning under $\frac{1}{4}$ inch and then edge stitching or use a machine embroidery stitch to provide a decorative edge and trim close to it. Along the other long edge run two rows of machine gathering and pull up the bobbin threads until the work is the required length (diagram 34). Neaten the thread ends securely. This type of ruffle is attached to a garment either forming right sides together with the gathered edges towards the lower part of the garment and the neatened edge towards the upper part of the garment. Stitch in position along the seam line then press the ruffle towards the lower part of the garment taking care not to flatten the gathers. Alternatively, this type of ruffle can be inserted into a seam.

Double ruffle This type of ruffle is gathered through the centre so that the ruffles are formed either side of the stitching. It can

31

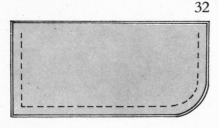

32

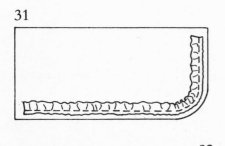

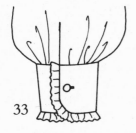

33

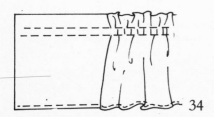

34

be formed in one of two ways so that the fabric will either be single thickness or double thickness. For single thickness fabric, neaten both long edges of the ruffle and gather it through the centre using two rows of gathers (diagram 35). The gathers are then drawn up and the wrong side of the ruffle is applied to the right side of the fabric and stitched through the centre. A ribbon can first of all be placed over the machine gathers and the ruffle top stitched into position through the ribbon. For a double thickness ruffle, cut the ruffle to the desired length and add twice the finished width. Working from the wrong side of the fabric, fold the raw edges towards the centre, wrong sides together and place two lines of machine gathers $\frac{1}{8}$ inch from each raw edge through the centre of the ruffle (diagram 36). Draw up the bobbin threads until the ruffle is of the required length and then pin wrong side down over the right side of the fabric. Top stitch into position with two lines of machine stitching. Remove gathering threads.

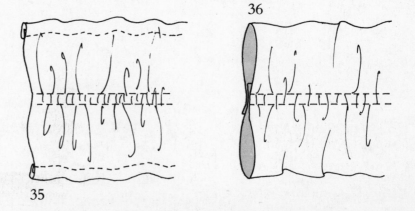

35   36

Circular ruffles This type of ruffle is often included into a commercial paper pattern. Learn how the pattern is formed so that you can cut them yourself to add to another garment. A circle is drawn on to a piece of tissue paper with its circumference equal to the desired finished length of the ruffle (diagram 37). Decide on the width for the ruffle, add $\frac{1}{2}$ inch for turnings and draw a further circle this distance outside the first Cut out the pattern, lay the tissue on the fabric cutting first of all round the outer circle and then around the inner circle. Cut a straight line through the circle and neaten edges. The widest edge and the two short edges, should be neatened with a narrow hem, hand or machine stitched. Stay stitch $\frac{1}{4}$ inch from the inside curve and then clip the curve to within $\frac{1}{16}$ inch of the stitching (diagram 38). With the right sides together and the bottom edge of the ruffle turned up, pin the stay stitching to the garment as required and stitch. The ruffle is then turned down and the stitching concealed. This provides particularly soft and pretty finished effect.

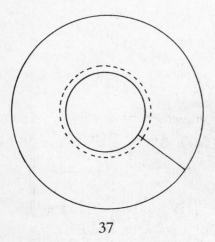

37

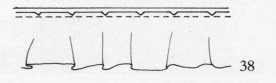

38

Simple trimming details add finish and flair

EMBROIDERY

If you first of all make your own clothes and home furnishings and afterwards embroider them, you can be sure of a truly original item which will really feature your own personality and ideas. You may find it easier to start on a small household item such as a napkin and progress to embroidering clothes afterwards. It may on first sight seem laborious and time consuming but a small taste of embroidery is usually enough to whet the appetite to do more and more adventurous designs. Normally, when you start hand stitching, you form a knot to hold the thread in position but with embroidery, you bring the needle up through the fabric leaving a thread on the wrong side. This can be held firm in your other hand to start with and later sewn in by running it under a few stitches. When you finish a thread, take it through to the wrong side of the work and draw it through a few stitches. Use strands of embroidery thread of medium length and do not pull your stitches too tight.

Embroidery stitches

Arrow head stitch It is used for light filling. Bring the needle through the right side of the fabric at the top left corner. Insert it below and to the right bringing it through to the right at the top line. Insert the needle back to the lower left next to the first stitch. The stitches form lines of 'V' shapes (diagram 1).

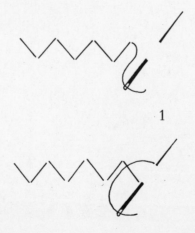

1

Back stitch Is the same stitch as you used for sewing and is not illustrated. It is a basic stitch used for lines, outlines and as a foundation for other stitches.

Blanket stitch It was used originally on blankets to bind the raw edges. In embroidery it is used as a decorative outline stitch, to cover raw edges or to make a flower when worked in a circle (diagram 2).

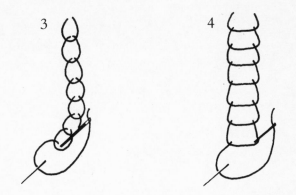

Chain stitch Can be used for outlining or filling when a number of rows are worked close together. Bring the needle to the right side of the fabric and hold the thread down with the left thumb, insert the needle back where the thread emerged and bring to the right side a short distance forward. Draw needle out over loop (diagram 3).

Open chain stitch This is useful as a garment trimming through which ribbon may be threaded. It is worked in a similar way to chain stitch except that the thread is inserted into fabric on the right side of the chain and a small stitch is made forward towards the left side of the chain (diagram 4).

Coral stitch A simple but effective method of outlining, worked from right to left. Bring needle to right side, hold thread in place with left thumb and make a small vertical stitch under the first part of the thread and over the second part of the thread as shown. Draw needle through to make a knot (diagram 5).

Couching This is another outline stitch which is often worked with two different threads. Place one thread along the line to be covered holding it down with the left hand and with another thread make tiny stitches at right angles over the laid thread and the fabric at even intervals. Bring all threads to the wrong side for neatening (diagram 6).

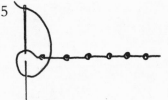

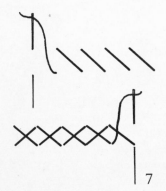

Cross stitch Starting at the lower left corner, make a diagonal stitch to the upper right corner by taking a vertical stitch. Continue across the line, working left to right, then turn and stitch from lower right to upper left over each stitch to form the cross. This stitch may be worked singly or in groups (diagram 7).

8

Feather stitch This is a decorative stitch which is worked from the top of the work downwards. Bring the needle out slightly to the left of the line to be covered, hold the thread down with the left thumb, make a slanting stitch to the right and a little below with the needle pointing to the left and draw the needle through over the thread. Carry the thread to the left side of the line and make a similar stitch with the needle pointing to the right (diagram 8).

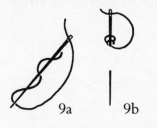

9a   9b

French knot Bring the needle to the right side where the knot is to be made, wind the thread two or three times around the needle point (diagram 9a), insert needle into fabric close to where the thread emerged and pull to the wrong side holding the twists in place (diagram 9b). The stitch is used extensively to embroider plain garments such as the yoke of a baby's or child's dress.

10

Herring-bone stitch or catch-stitch This stitch is worked over two lines. First take a stitch from right to left on the upper line, then take a similar stitch on the lower line to the right. The next stitch is again taken on the upper line to the right (diagram 10).

11

Holbein stitch Work a running stitch along the line to be covered keeping the stitches and spaces between, equal in length. A further line of running stitches is made back over the same line filling the empty spaces with stitches. This is a simple but effective outline stitch which is sometimes worked in two different coloured threads (diagram 11).

12

Lazy Daisy stitch This is a quick way to make flowers and petals. Bring the needle and thread to the right side in the centre of the flower, hold the thread down, insert the needle close to where the thread emerged, then bring up at bottom of the petal drawing the needle over the thread. Fasten down with a tiny stitch made over the loop (diagram 12).

13

Long and short stitch This is similar to satin stitch but alternate long and short stitches are taken for a textured effect. Two colours can be used to give a shaded effect and the stitch is used for filling and shading (diagram 13).

Outline stitch Work from left to right, bring needle to right side of the work slightly below the line. Take a short stitch inserting the needle slightly above the line and bring it back to the left slightly below. Stitches are formed at a very slight angle with the thread above the needle (diagram 14). If the stitch is made in the opposite way, it is termed 'Stem stitch'.

Running stitch This is the same stitch that is used for ordinary sewing. Insert the needle in and out of the fabric in straight or curved lines at regular intervals.

Laced running stitch Having made a line of running stitches, thread needle with another colour and thread the needle in and out of the running stitches without taking stitches in the actual fabric (diagram 15).

15

Satin stitch This is used to cover an area solidly. Bring the needle up at one edge of the design, down into the opposite edge, carry under the fabric bringing it up next to the original stitch. Stitches should be parallel but may be worked in a vertical, horizontal or diagonal direction (diagram 16).

16

Stem stitch Working from left to right, take the needle to the right side just above the line, take a small stitch from right to left inserting the needle slightly below the line and bringing it out above the line in the centre of the previous stitch. The thread is held below the needle and the stitch used for flower stems and markings (diagram 17).

17

Smocking This is a favourite form of decoration for children's clothes which from time to time enjoys a fashion success on adult garments as well. Ready to wear garments which feature smocking are usually very costly so by learning to smock yourself, you can save money and probably derive considerable enjoyment from it too. Fine fabrics are most suited to this type of work. Fabrics such as ginghams, spots or stripes are very easy to use as a result of their geometric design. If you use any other fabric, you will probably require a transfer. These can be purchased and if smocking is featured on a pattern envelope, the manufacturer will include the smocking transfer.

The work must first of all be gathered up and the success of the work depends upon the evenness of the gathering. This is done from the wrong side, using a separate thread for each row of gathering. Draw up the gathering threads to the required measurement and secure the gathering threads. Even out the gathers.

The smocking is made from the right side of the fabric using a crewel needle and three or more strands of embroidery thread.

14

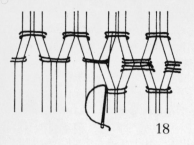

18

Each stitch is taken through a pleat formed by the gathers and the rows are used as a guide to keep the stitching straight. A very wide variety of stitches and designs can be worked to include honeycomb, diamond and cable smocking all of which are described here.

Honeycomb smocking This takes up less fabric than ordinary smocking stitches so only twice the width is required because the stitch has wide expansion. It is worked in double rows. First stitch two pleats together on the top row then take the needle to the lower row passing underneath the fabric and stitch together two pleats to include one from the first pair. Continue stitching up and down alternately, working two stitches over each pair of pleats, passing the thread on the wrong side of the work (diagram 18). When the two rows are complete, do another two rows in the same way.

Diamond smocking This smocking is worked like honeycomb except the thread is passed on the outside of the work. Work from one row of gathers to the other over two pleats keeping the thread below the needle when working the two stitches up to the top line and keeping it above the needle when working the two stitches down to the lower line (diagram 19). To complete the diamond pattern, repeat alternating the rows.

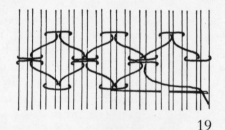

19

Cable smocking This stitch is worked on one row of dots but if a further row of dots is placed close to this, two separate rows can be worked to form a double cable smocking. Bring the needle up at the first dot and take a stitch at the next dot with the thread above the needle. In the next stitch, pass it below the needle and the next stitch above it and so on alternating across the work (diagram 20). Double cable stitch is worked on another row of dots placed very close and the stitches are worked by alternating the thread so that they meet the threads of the last row.

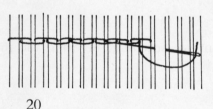

20

Appliqué This is a bold type of embroidery which is very quick and easy to do because it entails only a minimum amount of stitching. Designs are cut out from contrast fabric and applied to a background. It is advisable to select fabrics for your designs which do not ravel easily. Felt is a popular choice because it does not ravel at all. Appliqué can be worked in suedes and leathers as well. Although appliqué is generally regarded as a form of decoration, if clothes have suffered a hedge tear, mend the hedge tear first and then attach an appliqué shape over the tear for further strength and decoration.

By hand The motif is placed onto the garment and then using embroidery thread, blanket stitched all round to neaten the edge and hold the design firmly in position (diagram 21). Alternatively, you may prefer to cut out your appliqué shapes in finer fabric in which case it should be cut out in double thick-

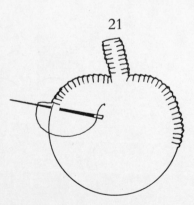

21

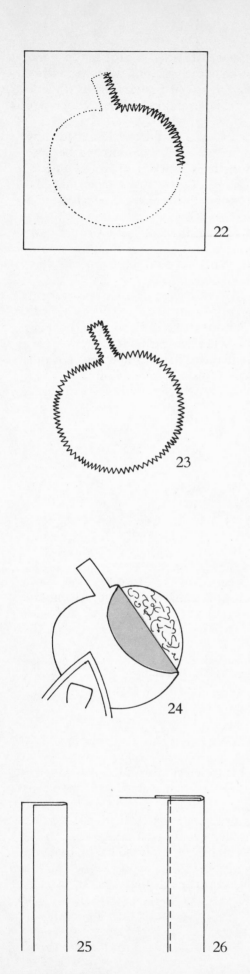

22

23

24

ness and the two seamed together right sides together leaving an opening through which the fabric can be turned, after the seams have been trimmed and clipped. Finish the opening and press and slip stitch onto the garment.

By machine A swing needle machine really comes into its own here and can save endless time. Trace a design onto your fabric which is to be used for the appliqué. Baste this fabric into position with the design correctly placed over the garment and then using the zig-zag stitch, machine stitch round the outside of the design on all sides and then remove (diagram 22). Neaten thread ends and then trim away the excess fabric up to the edges of the zig-zag stitching taking care not to clip into the stitching (diagram 23).

Iron-on appliqué A selection of motifs and designs are available that are ironed on to fabric to provide decoration (diagram 24). Alternatively, provided the appliqué fabric does not ravel, a bonding material such as fuseable fleece can be used. Always carefully follow the manufacturer's instructions for use.

Braid Braid can be used to decorative and functional use. A functional use is to bind the raw edge of a garment so that no facing is required, at the same time providing the garment with an attractive and decorative finish. Fold the braid along its length wrong sides together just off the centre line so that one side is slightly wider than the other (diagram 25). The widest side will be placed on the wrong side of the garment with the narrower side to the right side of the garment. Press the braid, then encase the raw edges holding it in position with pin basting or basting. Top stitch from the right side close to the edge of the braid through all thicknesses (diagram 26). By placing the slightly wider side of the braid on the wrong side of the garment, you can ensure that your stitching will encase all thicknesses. If the braid has to be continued round a corner, stitch to within an inch of the corner and then form a mitre on both the right and wrong sides by folding under the excess triangle of fabric. Continue stitching, pivoting the machine through 90 degrees at the corner.

Rick rack braid This is a simple braid which has been available for years and enjoys popularity for children's garments as well as adult clothing. It is put to excellent decorative effect if several widths are used in conjunction with one another around the hem of a skirt. Alternatively, it may be used to pick out design details such as pockets or yokes. To apply, lay the braid in position and straight stitch through its centre to the garment (diagram 27).

25

26

27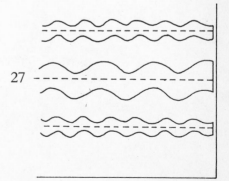

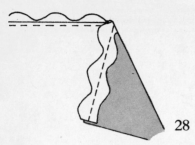

28

It may also be used as a decorative edging for the lower end of a sleeve or a hem. Turn the edge of the fabric which is to be trimmed to. the wrong side and press. Lay the braid on the wrong side so that only the points of one edge are visible and then working from the right side top stitch close to the folded edge of the fabric (diagram 28). Alternatively, the braid can be attached to the right side of a garment close to the finished folded edge and stitched through the centre.

Scallops This is a very attractive finish for the lower edge of a garment or it may be used for home furnishings to good advantage as well. The scallops may be already marked on your pattern in which case it is necessary to transfer the scallop lines to the fabric either by means of dressmaker's carbon paper and a tracing wheel or by placing the tissue pattern piece over the work and actually stitching through the line on the tissue through to the fabric and its facing. This latter method will mean that you are unable to use the pattern again because the tissue pattern must be torn away either side of the stitching afterwards. It is usual to transfer the scallop line to the facing then stitch along this line through both thicknesses using 15–20 stitches per inch, forming a smooth curved line (diagram 29).

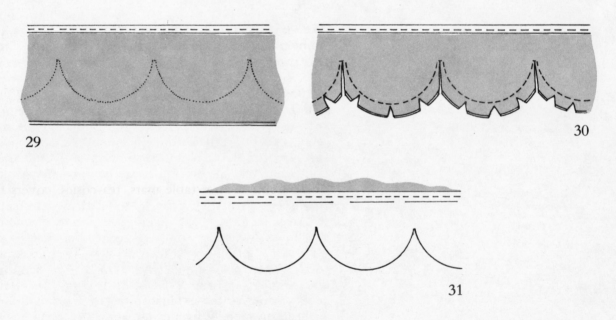

29

30

31

At the points, take one or two small stitches straight across before commencing the next curve. This will considerably facilitate the process of turning the scallops through afterwards. If interfacing has been used, it should be trimmed very close to the stitching line and the garments seams thereafter trimmed to $\frac{1}{4}$ inch and clipped (diagram 30). Clip very carefully up to the stitching at the points taking care that the stitching is not caught. Turn the facing to the wrong side and press out the edges of the scallops first on the facing side and then on the garment. To make sure that this edge will not roll after the garment has been laundered or dry-cleaned, make small prick stitches through from the facing to the seam allowance making sure that the garment fabric is not caught-in (diagram 31). The facing now forms a hem and is hemmed up.

182

SEWING
FOR
THE HOME

The same ideas, techniques and fashion can be brought to your home to give your furnishings a look of quality, with economy and most important of all, with originality. It seems strange that, in a society which buys so much fabric by the yard for the purpose of making clothes, that more furnishing fabric is not bought for the purpose of making things for the home. Until recently there was an excellent excuse, in that pattern companies were involved only with the garment trade but now realising the need for fashion and originality at home these pattern companies are producing patterns for almost every need. Small items such as table mats, tea-cosies, covers for toasters or mixers and napkins can be sewn from remnants of fabric left over from garment making. It is an area where appliqué, machine embroidery and hand embroidery can be put to very good use. Curtains are a must in every home and we are well used to the long drapes which frame our windows by day covering them by night. These have always been fairly easy to make thanks to the explicit instructions of the manufacturers of heading tape. Why not use a valance on your window to cover the curtain heading or cover a pelmet with matching or contrasting fabric? In the bedroom, make a skirt for your dressing table in a variety of finishes or simply cover a bedside table with a circular table-cloth. Accessories for cupboards and wardrobes in the form of 'organisers' are available as patterns so that you can hang your shoes on the back of a cupboard door, store your handbags neatly away in slots. Instructions for padding clothes hangers so that they do not harm your garments – all these are wonderful space savers. Beds need bed-spreads or maybe you use a duvet in which case why not make the duvet cover for yourself and adapt your sheets to become fitted sheets. Even the bathroom is a place for fashion and individuality with covers for your tissue boxes and wastepaper basket, seat covers and mats.

183

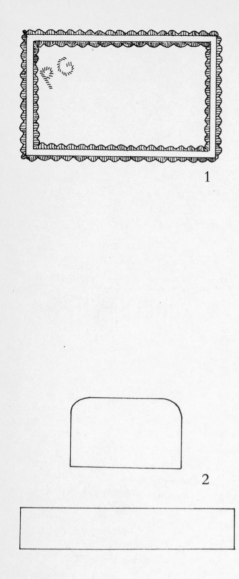

1

2

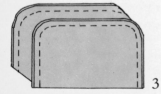

3

The temptation is there and if you feel unwilling or unable to undertake the task unaided, you are now able to purchase a pattern which will quote you accurate instructions for making up and yardaging and haberdashery requirements.

Kitchen and dining-room accessories

It is always easier to make a start on smaller items and this is a particularly useful place to start because in some cases, you will be able to use fabric remnants. Table mats and napkins are usually a necessity. A napkin is made from a square of fabric and the outside edges neatened by folding the raw edge under and then refolding and top stitching through from the right side close to the edge. Raw edges can also be neatened with a zig-zag but a decorative embroidery stitch worked on a machine would be preferable. A scalloped edge formed on the machine is particularly attractive and the fabric is afterwards trimmed away to the scalloped edge. For a total effect run another line of machine embroidery inside this around all four sides. Choose a machine embroidery stitch which will complement the scallop at the edge. Reverse the scallops, for instance, so that the straight edges run nearest to each other with the rounded edges furthest away from each other (diagram 1). Table place mats can be made in exactly the same manner in the same fabric or a total contrast. These can repeat the exact design details on a rectangle. For each member of the family, you could work their initials in satin stitch on one place mat and one napkin of each set. Don't forget to allow a few spares without initials for visitors. A toaster cover or mixer cover is an enormous help in the kitchen. It enables you to keep the appliance out on a shelf and ready for use without risking dust. If the cover is made in a brightly coloured fabric or features a bright design detail, this will enhance the look of your kitchen as well as serving a useful purpose. Two sides will be required plus a strip to cover the ends and run across the top of the appliance. The size can easily be measured by placing a piece of card or stiff paper beside the appliance and marking the outer size onto it. The cover should be made 1 inch larger all round and allow the usual $\frac{5}{8}$ inch seam turning. You will have one pattern piece for the side of which you must cut two pieces of fabric and a further pattern piece in the shape of a strip (diagram 2). The long edge of the strip should be equal in length to the seamline of the curved edge of the side. With right sides together, pin and stitch these two edges together and repeat the other side (diagram 3). It is not normal when making such items to neaten raw edges in any way other than forming welt or flat felled seams. Here a flat felled seam can be formed by trimming the seam allowance from the strip to $\frac{1}{8}$ inch and pressing the seam allowance from the side over towards the strip. Turn under $\frac{1}{8}$ inch and stitch through all thicknesses in the normal way.

Curtains/Draperies These are often made by sewing the upper edge of the fabric onto a tape which is then gathered to form the type of pleating required. It is very important to prepare the fabric carefully before cutting such that the edges are at right angles to the selvedge. If the fabric is woven evenly, straighten the edges by pulling a thread and cutting along this line. More than one width may be required for each curtain in which case two pieces of fabric are joined together down the length. It is not necessary to cut the selvedges off but make diagonal snips into them to prevent puckering. If patterned fabric is selected, it is essential to measure the total length of the pattern and allow extra when calculating the yardage required. Most large stores have qualified staff who will advise you accurately as to the amount of fabric required, provided you have the accurate measurements of the window and know which type of tape you plan to use. Larger seam turnings are allowed for curtains so allow $1\frac{1}{4}$ inches for each seam and $1\frac{1}{2}$ inches at each side for the hem. It is also necessary to allow extra length for the lower hems and the headings but this varies with the different types of tape.

Curtains/draperies can be lined or unlined but a better draping effect is achieved with lined curtains. If preferred, detachable linings can be sewn but these use their own tape and are stitched quite separately. The method allows the lining to be detached quickly and easily for washing or dry-cleaning separately.

Conventional headings These are basic gathered curtains which use standard tape in cotton or nylon so that the tape can be matched to your fabric (diagram 4). When using this type of tape, the curtains should measure one and a half times the width of the window at least. A fuller more gathered effect is achieved if more fabric is used. Allow 2 inches for the heading and 4 inches for the hem. As an example to help you calculate the yardage required, for a window measuring 5 foot wide and 3 foot 6 in length, the minimum amount of curtain width that should be used is 5 feet plus 2 foot 6 ($1\frac{1}{2}$ times the width) which equals 7 feet 6 inches. Furnishing fabric is normally sold in 48 inch widths which is 4 feet. Remembering that $1\frac{1}{2}$ inches is required each side of each curtain for the side hems, the 7 foot 6 required for the curtain width plus the 6 inches for hems is exactly equal to 8 feet. You will therefore require two widths of fabric. The finished length of the curtain is to be 3 foot 6 inches and to this you must allow the extra 6 inches required for the heading and hem so that it equals 4 feet. As two fabric widths are required your total curtain length in a plain fabric will be 8 feet which is approximately $2\frac{3}{4}$ yards. Remember that if you are using a patterned fabric, it will be necessary to allow extra yardage to match the pattern.

Pencil pleats These are achieved by using a different type of tape which is deeper and gathered up along both edges (diagram 5). It forms even folds of fabric across the width of each curtain and the folds are of course deeper. To use this type of heading, you will require at least $2\frac{1}{4}$ times the width of the curtain track plus allowance for seams and side hems. You will still need to allow 4 inches for the hem and 4 to 6 inches for the heading.

Tall conventional headings If you have no pelmets, and find that it is the tall heading which provides a neat finish at the upper end of the curtain which you require, tape can be purchased which is considerably wider than the conventional tape but as it is gathered up in the usual manner, it is not extravagant on fabric (diagram 6). You should allow $1\frac{1}{2}$ times the width of the curtain track plus seam and side hem allowances. Greater fullness will of course provide a softer finished effect. Still allow 4 inches for the hem with 4 inches for the heading.

Pinch pleats These are formed by using a deep heading tape in conjunction with special curtain hooks which actually pleat the fabric (diagram 7). You can use single, double or triple pleats

4

5

6

7

and the amount of fabric you require, depends on the type of pleating you plan to use. You will need to add 4 inches to the length for the heading and 4 inches for the lower hem but to estimate accurately for the amount of fabric that you require, contact the manufacturer of the heading tape who will supply you accurate conversion tables for pleating. As a very rough guide, if you use 48 inch width fabric to form triple pleats, you will require approximately double the width of your curtain track. This however, is only a very rough guide and you should always buy your fabric from accurate measurements on the advice of the manufacturer of the heading tape or an experienced sales assistant.

If the curtains are to be lined, the lining is tucked underneath the tape at the top of the curtain, the selvedges folded under along the sides and the linings hemmed down on to the side hems of the curtains. At the lower edge, the curtain fabric can be taken-up on to the lining as with a dress which has an under-lining or both hems can be taken up separately and the fabrics caught loosely together at the sides. You will normally need about the same amount of lining material as curtain material for this type of lining or detachable linings. As you do not need to allow for headings or pattern matching, it is sometimes possible to reduce the yardage a little.

Net curtains The amount of fabric you need to purchase, is entirely dependent upon your choice of fabric. If you are using an absolutely plain net fabric, you should allow at least $2\frac{1}{2}$ times the width of your curtain track but a more decorative net may only require to be $1\frac{1}{2}$ times the width of the curtain track. Accept the advice of the sales assistant and use the special heading tape for net curtains.

Points to remember Even nowadays, it is possible for furnishing fabrics to shrink so unless you are using a man made fibre that you know will not shrink, allow an inch per yard extra to insure against this.

With all tapes, which have cords to form the pleats, do not cut the cord after it is drawn up because when curtains are cleaned, it is advisable to release the gathers or pleats to ensure satisfactory cleaning. Rely on the manufacturer of the fabric as to whether the fabric will need dry cleaning or washing.

You may like to add ruffles along your pelmets in which case you use your dressmaking knowledge to stitch the ruffle to the desired length and width but when attaching the ruffle to the pelmet, remember that it must be removable at a later date for cleaning. You may like to consider using a touch and close fastener which can be glued with an adhesive to the pelmet and stitched to the wrong side of your ruffle (diagram 8). Another idea for covering pelmets is to form scallops at the lower edge. You will require one strip of fabric which will show and a further facing of equivalent length. Form the scallops at the lower edge in the usual manner and then stitch the two pieces of fabric together, leaving an opening through which the whole pelmet cover can be turned. Press and fasten the opening with slip stitches from the right side and then the pelmet cover can be attached to the pelmet. Again, it is import-ant to remember that it will need to be detachable for cleaning.

Bathrooms

Bathroom sets can be readily purchased in the shops consisting

8

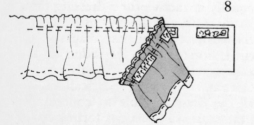

of seat covers, and mats. It is also possible to buy covers for tissue boxes, dressing-table boxes and wastepaper baskets. If you use your ingenuity, here is another room in which you can put your personal ideas into operation. Use heavy paper to form a pattern for the item which is to be covered and trace its exact shape. When cutting-out the fabric, remember always to allow $\frac{5}{8}$ inch outside this point for seam turnings. Alternatively, leave somebody else to do that side of the hard work and when you have purchased your pattern, simply follow the instruction sheet to form the items you require.

Bedrooms

The potential is endless and the choice of co-ordinating fabrics exciting. Obey the rule of starting simply and make a circular table cover adding a touch of femininity to a bedside table. Of course this type of table cover is equally suitable for a table in any room of the house provided the fabric is adapted to suit the room. The diameter of the circle will need to be the diameter of the table top plus twice the desired length to which the table-cloth is to hang at the side of the table. The measurement can of course be enormous and unless your fabric is particularly wide, it may be necessary to piece the fabric by forming a seam. You can make a pattern for this item by halving the diameter of the cloth. This measurement will be the radius of the circle and you can draw it out on a large piece of paper. If this will not fit onto your fabric, cut the pattern piece as required remembering always to add $\frac{5}{8}$ inch seam turnings for seaming. The method for finishing the cloth is a matter of personal choice. If the fabric chosen is sufficiently brightly patterned, no decoration will be required and a simple turned hem can be formed. Alternatively the raw edge can be neatened with a machine embroidery stitch. A simple machined hem can be formed at the lower edge of a plain cloth and fringing or braid attached. Further lines of braid or trimming can then be applied to the cloth as desired.

Dressing-table A dressing-table should always look feminine and glamorous and one of the easiest ways to do this is to make a dressing table skirt and top. For a square dressing-table, it will be necessary to cut one pattern piece for the top and a further strip which will be equal in length to all four sides of the dressing-table. Seam the two together so that they form a kind of hat for the top of your dressing table and then if you wish braid or lace can be attached to the lower edge of the hat to frame a gathered or pleated skirt. To make a pleated skirt, form box pleats and baste in position. The pleated heading can then be either stitched right sides together with the upper hat and the seam line trimmed thereafter or if the hat is to be kept separate, attached to a heading tape (diagram 9). If a heading tape is used, the pleated skirt will form a kind of curtain which will need to run on curtain track, and open up to provide a knee hole. A gathered skirt is equally attractive for a dressing table and can be made in exactly the same way as curtains by allowing $1\frac{1}{2}$ times the width of the curtain track at least (diagram 10). The upper edge of the skirt is hooked onto the sliders on the curtain track to allow it to open and close freely. In this instance a separate hat with a lace edging or maybe with scallops can be placed over the top of the dressing table to conceal the upper part of the skirt. In the same way you can form a cover

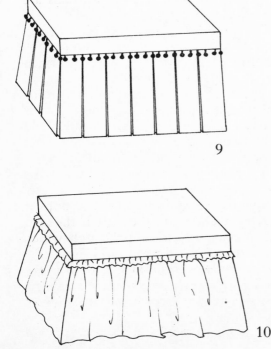

9

10

for your dressing table stool to match.

Accessories Space savers for your wardrobe are a marvellous idea and in addition to being economical with the space in your wardrobe, they provide an easy method of locating a particular object. Shoe-holders which usually attach to the back of your cupboard or wardrobe door have pockets into which the toes of your shoes will slide and this avoids the floor space of the cupboard being unnecessarily cluttered. It also means that when you wish to wear a particular pair of shoes, they can be easily spotted and removed. Handbags can also be slotted away into compartments of a handbag holder and then hung up alongside your clothes. Consult the accessories section of your pattern catalogue for patterns for space saving ideas. Such items can be made yourself, without the aid of a pattern but will be much quicker with its help.

Bedspreads If the bedspread is for a single bed, it will be possible to cover the top part of the bed without seaming the fabric and then attach to it a gathered or pleated frill to form the sides. For a double bed however, it will be necessary to seam the fabric unless you have managed to obtain it in an exceptionally wide width. Run the fabric through the centre of the bed such that the seam instead of being formed at the centre is formed at either side of the bed parallel to the sides (diagram 11). Again it is not normal to form an open seam but to make all seams welt or flat felled seams. Occasionally when a very fine fabric is used, a french seam can be formed.

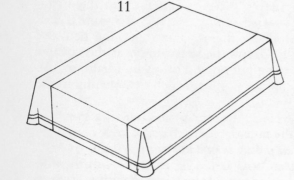

11

Estimating the amount of fabric which you will require, is similar to the method used in establishing curtain yardages. First of all you will need to know how many widths of fabric you require to fit the width and height of the bed. As an example, if your bed measures 4 foot 6 inches wide and 18 inches high and 6 feet long, it is immediately obvious that you will require more than one fabric width of 48 inches to go across the bed and down its sides. The total measurement at this point is 4 foot 6 plus two times 18 inches which equals 7 feet 6 inches. Two widths of fabric will measure 8 feet and the extra 6 inches will accommodate seam turnings and hems and two fabric widths are required. To the length of the bed, 6 feet, add 18 inches for the fall at the bottom of the bed plus a further allowance for tucking in around the pillow. 18 inches should be sufficient. The total length will be 6 feet plus twice 18 inches (36) equalling 9 feet or 3 yards but remember as two fabric widths are required this is doubled to 6 yards.

To make this bedspread, split one fabric width in half, and keep the other whole. Attach the raw edges of the lengths which have been cut in half to the selvedges of the piece which remained whole and in this way your seams will be formed approximately 6 inches from the side edges of the bed. A hem should be formed right around the bedspread and if required, a trimming can be attached.

Another type of bedspread can feature a plain fitted top with a gathered skirt in which case lengths of fabric are cut to the desired depth, plus an allowance for seam turning and hem and gathered up before being attached to the top covering (diagram 12). This type of bed cover can be used for either a double or single bed but on a single bed no seaming will be necessary across the top cover. For a double bed, form seams

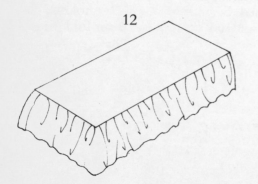

12

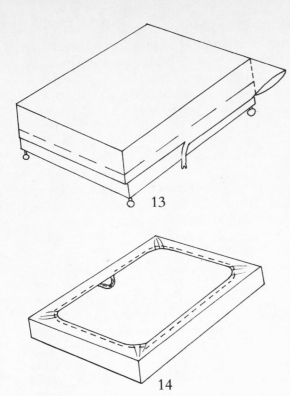

13

14

as before so that they are well sited. Never have a centre seam.

Seam lines on home furnishings of this variety can easily be made into a design detail if they are covered with attractive braid.

Fitted sheets Maybe you already have some sheets which can be made into fitted sheets to save you time when bed making and always ensure that the sheet is well tucked-in. Alternatively fabric by the yard can be purchased. Lay the sheet over the mattress right side upper-most and at the four corners, form a seam as indicated (diagram 13). Mark a line 4 inches below the bottom of the mattress and trim away the excess fabric below this point. Remove the sheet from the bed stitching the four corner seams. Reduce seam turnings to $\frac{1}{8}-\frac{1}{4}$ inch and form french seams with fabric wrong sides together. Make a narrow machined hem right around the lower edge of the sheet leaving an opening to insert a narrow piece of elastic. Insert the elastic to run through the hem with a safety pin. At this stage it will probably be necessary to put the sheet back on the bed and test to see that the elastic draws the sheet under at the corners whilst still allowing it to be put on and off easily (diagram 14). Firmly stitch the elastic in position and stitch the opening in the narrow hem.

Duvet covers These are even simpler to make than a standard pillow case. They usually take the form of a rectangle of double fabric which may fasten either at one end with a slight overlap and a button and button hole fastening or more simply still, down one side leaving an opening which is tied with matching tapes. You will already know the size of your duvet and to this you should add 1 foot for every 3 feet. If the duvet measures 6 feet by 3 feet across your cover should measure 8 feet by 4 feet. This is to accommodate the fullness of the feathers as they expand with the heat. As a duvet cover will need to be laundered frequently, french seams would be advisable so having cut your two pieces of fabric to the required measurement having already seamed them if necessary, place the fabrics wrong sides together and take a seam of $\frac{1}{4}$ to $\frac{3}{8}$ inch leaving an opening down one side approximately 30 inches long. Trim seam turnings to $\frac{1}{8}$ inch except along the open edges and then turning the fabric right sides together, stitch $\frac{1}{4}$ inch from the stitched edge. Along the open edges, turn $\frac{1}{8}$ inch to the wrong side of fabric and edge stitch, catching in the tapes at even intervals on both sides (diagram 15).

A button and buttonhole opening would always be formed at the lower edge of a duvet. The upper part of the cover, folds towards the lower part for about an inch and is then lapped by the lower cover. Both are folded edges with 1 inch folded back and the raw edges neatened. Form machine buttonholes in the upper fold (lower cover) and sew buttons on lower fold (upper cover).

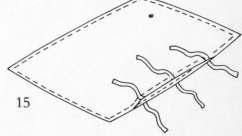

15

INDEX

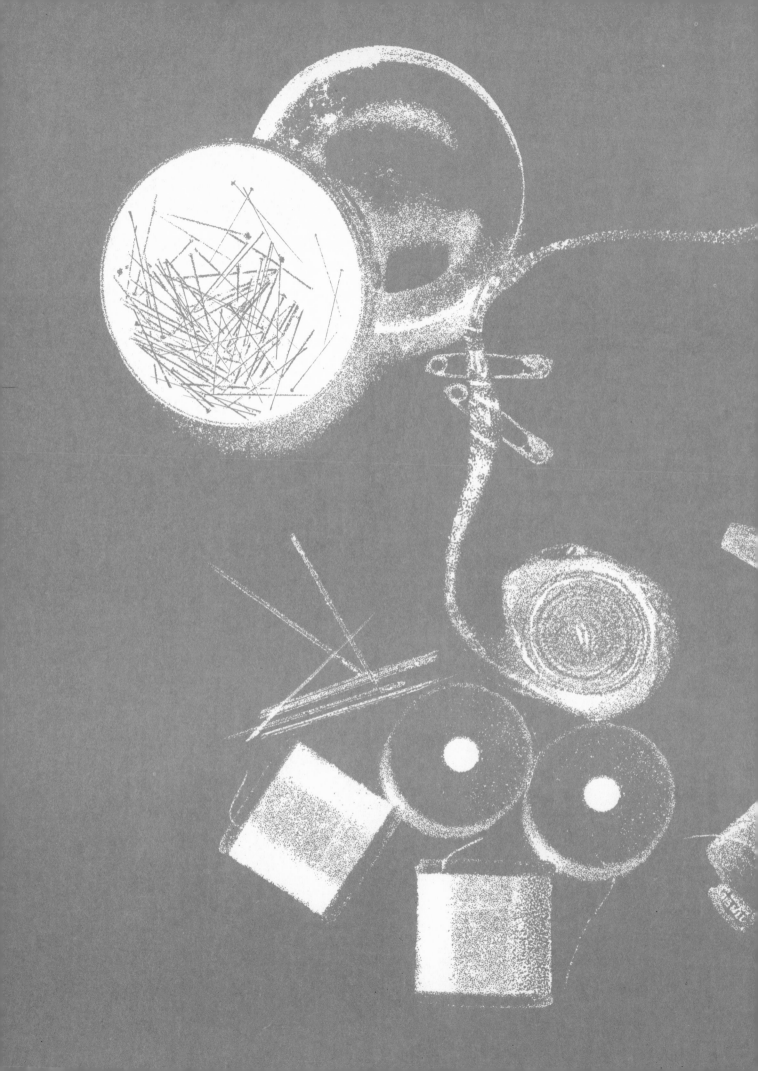